MAN
ON THE
GOAT TRAIL

T. ISOM, SR.

MAN
IN THE
SAFARI SUIT

authorHOUSE®

AuthorHouse™
1663 Liberty Drive
Bloomington, IN 47403
www.authorhouse.com
Phone: 1 (800) 839-8640

Published by AuthorHouse 09/07/2017

ISBN: 978-1-5462-0733-7 (sc)
ISBN: 978-1-5462-0732-0 (e)

Library of Congress Control Number: 2017913766

Print information available on the last page.

King James Version (KJV)
Public Domain

CONTENTS

Dedication

To God be the glory for the inspiration in my life. He has anointed me as a spiritual surgeon to operate on the hearts and minds of men. Wherefore I dedicate this book to my Lord and Savior Jesus Christ, in whom I'm deeply grateful.

I also dedicate this book to my lovely wife Toshya L. Isom. Who's truly a gifted prophet and also the author of Toolbox of Life. She's a woman full of experience who's proven to be invaluable in my life. She's dedicated, full of integrity and a true example for the millennial woman in Gods kingdom.

To the greatest woman I know someone who has stood with me through thick and thin, a true woman of God my mother Dorothy M. Isom. God has used her to be an anchor in my life. She's a true prayer warrior who has fought by my side, believed in the God in my life and has been an avid supporter, as she's dedicated over fifty years of her life to mentoring women throughout the world.

I would like to give a special thanks to my six wonderful children Cassaundra, Rashanda, Tawanda, Kiana, Tyrone Jr. and Brandon for their unwavering support.

Introduction

Why do some kings in certain tribes check the history and back ground on those who are trying to be a part of their tribe? And quiet as its kept most of us look for the best when it comes to our family and our children. Most of us check the history of physical health, mental behavior and educational background because things transfer into the genes in the natural as well as the spiritual and are cultivated into your life style.

Let's talk about biological inheritance. Biological inheritance is what comes from your parents and what is going from you to your children. Can a family's biological nature be traced? Sure it can. Every family has a genetic identity made up of a unique group of genes. People talk on genetics all the time when they say it runs in the family. News flash it's the same in the spiritual realm. Spirits follow families for generations. There're things that your ancestors may have done that only the power of God can break. This is called a generational curse and yes it comes in all packages. Did you know that money can be a curse? How your family obtained the money is key and the spirit of the character you developed under the power of that money in your upbringing.

I heard someone say God has a sense of humor. If you don't believe it, the next time you go to the zoo look at a giraffe or hippopotamus or just simply look in the mirror. We are what we are whether born rich or born poor. So no matter how lopsided the cake may be when it comes out the oven. Cut it even, cover it with icing and nobody will ever know the difference. Only you will know what it took to make it look like that and if you don't tell they will never know. We live with ourselves each day seeking our way through life as we search for answers so that we may come to some understanding of our why.

Chapter 1

GENETICS

The Man on the Goat Trail and the Man in the Safari Suit describes two different men in the same environment, the jungle. The Man on the Goat Trail is wearing a coat made from goat skin; he's a hunter with a hands on style, as he sets traps to catch his prey. When he catches his prey he builds a fire, takes out his huge knife, skins his prey and rolls the meat over the fire. When his meat is ready he eats with his knife and hands using the skin of the prey to make coats and blankets. The Man in the Safari Suit travels in the jungle with servants and tribes men who guide him through the jungle carrying his equipment and riffle. When they spot a prey they hand him his riffle with a scope attached, and he kills his prey. The servants skin the prey, dress it and cook it in a skillet over the fire. He eats with a knife and fork in the jungle hanging the skin of the prey as a trophy on his wall for bragging rights. The bible says in Genesis 25:23, "And the Lord said unto her, two nations are in thy womb, and two manner of people shall be separated from thy bowels;" Here we have two different characters in one woman. Somebody will get a gene that the other won't have. Genesis 25:27-28, says "and the boys grew and Esau was a cunning hunter, a man of the field: and Jacob a plain man dwelling in tents." "And Isaac loved Esau, because he did eat of his venison: But Rebekah loved Jacob." Remember one womb yet two manner of people, Esau the Man on the Goat Trail and Jacob the Man in the Safari Suit. This is amazing two different natures cultivated differently. Isaac molded the character and spirit of Esau as a rough man's man an outdoorsman. Rebekah identified with Jacobs character as a clean cut inside man who's looking for opportunities. The deceitful attribute that dwelled within Jacob Rebekah molded and influenced through the spirit of social opportunity. These spirits travel with some bad friend's called seduction, greed, lust, murder and control. We all know God is in control and has set his will. The bible says in Romans 8:30, "More over whom he did predestinate, them he also called: and whom he called, them he also justified: and whom he justified, them he also glorified." Now that man has finally come into the knowledge and understanding of DNA we should advance our understanding to these facts. In the DNA of a person there are strains. These genes hold the genetic makeup of a person and this is how the person's character shows up. Once the character or attribute shows up it can be developed because it's in their blood, it just needs to be nurtured and heightened into its highest state. The spirit you house shows in your character whether it's good or bad. The spirit of a person may seem similar but there are no two spirits just alike, because they have their own makeup just as DNA. We have a natural DNA and a spiritual DNA. The natural is made up of complex cells and forms an individual's unique DNA. So the spirit of man is formed by the influencing of characters. Daniel said in Daniel 7:15, "My spirit in the midst of my body." Your body possesses your spirit. You see a child when he or she is born and you say they look just like their father and depending on their father's character it's either good or bad to you. Their father's upbringing formed his character and the father's spirit reflects his upbringing. Did you know your spirit can be sad if you're around someone who's always sad? Just as if you're around someone who's always negative, it will affect your spirit. A child is fragile and though that child has its own spirit and there spirit isn't evil. If that child grows up surrounded by evil it becomes an imprint on their spirit, which is a spiritual cell. If they come up around violence, fighting, arguing and cursing it becomes a part of their spirit because they don't know any better. The spirit of that child sees it as normal to fight or use vulgar language because it's a part of their upbringing and spiritual DNA. As a result the child's character has become ruined because of the surrounding spirits in the house. Damage is done to ones spirit if they're molested or raped. This experience will change their spirit because it becomes an imprint on their soul. As a result of the experience their character changes as it becomes molded by evil that only wants to destroy them or make their spirit sad, negative, violent and permissive. This forms a spiritual DNA making them a victim of their experience. Did you know demons will target you and try to imprint something on you? That's why older people say watch the company you keep. Yes, you must watch the company you keep because they will become a part of your spiritual DNA and your parent will began to say you're starting to act just like your friends. How? You didn't use to curse, but now every other word coming out your mouth is a curse word, you weren't thinking about sex, but now you want to give up your virginity, you didn't use to steal, but you stole it. You've allowed their spirit to influence you and these spirits aren't playing they mean business and will pull you deeper. Did you know that you're a target for Satan? You must understand that the world is designed against the child of God and Satan is trying to entrap every soul he can. Jesus said in ST. John 7:7, "The world cannot hate you: but me it hated, because I testify of it, that the works thereof are evil." Here Jesus is saying the world is trying to win you and gain your love. It hates me because I exposed it through the spirit of truth and when you receive this truth it will hate you as well. 1 John 2:15, states "So love not the world neither the things that are in the world, if any man love the world, the love of the father is not in him." If you truly love God you seek to please him and your nature and desires change as your spirit becomes one with his spirit. The presence of God will heal your heart from all the hurt and pain that you've been through, which has caused you to have low self-esteem or the feeling of insecurity because you were around someone who mentally abused you. My point is, when you're young the experiences you have shape your spirit and create your character. Parents you must be very protective of who you allow around your children or who's influencing them. The bible say's in 1 Timothy 4:1, "Now the spirit speaketh expressly, that in the latter times some shall depart from the faith, giving heed to seducing spirits, and doctrines of devils." Seducing spirits have had generation after generation to perfect their game and to get you caught up through social pressure and opportunities that require sacrifice. Notice the scripture said doctrines of devils. Satan's plan is to stop you by sending one among you who will talk a little but twist a lot in the word. They're so many different beliefs in the world people don't know what to believe anymore. The church has become worldly and confused. You can sit in a congregation of one hundred people, tell them to open their bible and get ten different interpretations of the same scripture due to the different versions of the bible. A man was talking about the bible; he was such a bible student but when the woman quoted a scripture from the KJV he said what was that? Is that in the bible? You see his bible read different and that's the plan of Satan. If he can't stop you he will confuse you to keep you from being on one accord. These are you're false prophets in the church. They have the appeal mixed with charisma and tell you it's ok to commit sin. No! It's not ok to commit sin. (Remember what happened to Adam and Eve) How did man get so far from God? Did his disobedience cause such a separation? Or did something happen during the separation? I began to think on several different theories that could be possible. One theory I have goes back to the war in heaven. Satan got uplifted thinking he knew as much as God knew and drew a following. It has been noted that a third of the angels in heaven turned with Satan against God. The bible tells us Michael and his warriors cast Satan and his followers out of Gods heaven. The bible says woe unto the inhabitants of the earth because this evil has come to earth in the realm of man, Gods precious creation. We know Satan and his fallen angels had one thing in mind, to get God back. So Satan and his followers needed a short and long term plan but how? They were cast out of heaven to earth where God had created man in his image and God loved man. I imagine Satan and his angels had one plan in mind, to turn Gods precious against him. Keep in mind Satan and the fallen angels were from a realm where time was different, a thousand years was as one day. Not only that, the fallen angels manifested themselves from the invisible to visible. Satan and the fallen angels understood the science of so many things because they came from heaven. The fallen angels understood man was Gods master piece and he could reproduce himself with woman. Angels can't reproduce themselves but they can corrupt the seed and genes in man. In this theory Satan's plot must have been to turn man immediately by getting him to disobey God. Satan working through the woman getting to Adam in the short term and in the long term the fallen angels planted corrupt and perverted seeds in the DNA of woman, which would continue to cultivate in the human body generation after generation. These demons never die; their plan is to damn man and take as many as they can to hell with this perverted gene. Man has been tampered with, especially his woman being a vessel to carry the long term plan of the gene which will cause a man to murder, steal, lie, to seek pleasure in another man, men with men, women with women and we know this is not Gods way because there is no fault in God! These demons are serious about the seed they planted and have every intension to carry it through till the end. Man has become wickeder and wiser now that he finally understands DNA. Fifty years ago he didn't have a clue but now we have finally come into the game with open and wiser minds. Yet Satan and his fallen angels still have a head start, because these spirits have been around since the beginning. Remember they were cast down from heaven and being from heaven their realm is far more advanced. This is why we need the help of Christ our Lord. I understand now more than ever when they say Satan is the prince of this world because Satan has infiltrated the relationship and purity of man with God. This is why there has to be so much atoning to God. The fallen angels planted their seed through the blood of woman and once those fallen angels planted that corrupt seed in woman it was over and they knew it. The book of Genesis the six chapter talks about the sons of God. "That the sons of God saw the daughters of man that they were fair, and they took them wives of all which they choose." Yes. Fallen angels that took on human flesh saw these beautiful women and started there long term plan with them by having sexual intercourse with them. If this wasn't in the bible you would think someone made it up. No! This is true. Woman who is a powerful and sensuous being has now been embraced by a supernatural being. Yes. Woman was intimate with fallen angels as she received and absorbed the corruption of the fallen angel's seed inside her womb. The thrust she must have felt during the time of impregnation, as she now carries the seed of a fallen angels DNA. This DNA will never die and can still be activated in the right setting. Here we have the woman as the host; the carrier of the DNA of the fallen angel who sinned against God by indulging with strange flesh. This tells us there is serious perversion in that DNA. Did you know that spirits never die? Just like dogs can sniff out cocaine, so can an evil spirit sniff out its kindred and kind to activate, cultivate and influence the resurgence of this type of activity. As a result women had children by fallen wicked angels as well as by men. It was because of this great sin Genesis 6:6, "And it repented the Lord that he had made man on earth, and it grieved him at his heart." These evil spirits in flesh had sex with human woman and the outcome was giants. The fallen angels had time on their side as they waited to cultivate their evil seeds through influence. This is why demons are always oppressing which is one of their main tactics. They know that you are born in sin because they changed the game by shaping you in iniquity. As they try to take you to hell; because they are bitter and hateful for being kicked out of heaven and knowing that you were created in the image of God. Satan and his fallen angels couldn't stand to see the pure heart of Adam with no sin walking in the cool of the day. So getting Adam cast out of the Garden of Eden was Satan's first phase. One of Satan key strategies is to divide and conquer. God was disappointed in Adam and we all know Adam blamed it on Eve. So God cast them out of the garden away from the tree of life. Just as he had the arch angel Michael to cast Satan and his fallen out of heaven. Now the fallen angels had man just where they wanted him. Where they could freely tamper with the woman to lead, guide and infect man with sin, using the woman as a host. This was the introduction of sin. The bible says in Romans 1:29-31, "Being filled with all unrighteousness, fornication, wickedness, covetousness, maliciousness: full of envy, murder, debate, deceit, malignity: whispers, backbiters, haters of God, despiteful, proud, boasters, inventors of evil things, disobedient to parents, without understanding, covenant breakers, without natural affection, implacable and unmerciful." After reading that, you can see those fallen angels were all that and more. They began to whisper in heaven against God and some even debated if they should be disobedient to their creator. By breaking the covenant because Satan being proud and boastful was envious of God and was backbiting against God every chance he got. Satan himself orchestrated an evil plot to take over heaven but Satan didn't understand how powerful God was and his plan failed. So Satan and his fallen angels brought it to earth by changing realms from invisible to visible. So they could infect man with this perversion by introducing their evil DNA into woman and nurturing it with demonic influence assuring the success of these evil genes as a part of their plot to destroy man and take souls to hell. As a result of Satan and his fallen angels intermingling their DNA with woman, man had become entangled with evil, causing kleptomaniacs, compulsive liars, nymphomaniacs, homosexuality, and murderers. Social sin is the most powerful sin because it operates through love, passion and emotions. Once Satan and his fallen angels got the advantage over man he made sure man became entangled with the sins of flesh. In this homosexuality became the ticking time bomb. The fallen Angels had sex with men and women. Could this also be how men with men and women with women came about? Could it be something to a homosexual saying it's in my genes? This type of lifestyle is passed on and becomes a powerful spirit and gene. Think about Sodom and Gomorrah. It was so wicked God had to destroy it but the spirit moves on and the DNA is passed on and can skip a generation or two. Take this for example, a husband and wife can have six children some can be bright yellow and another can be pistol black with blue eyes and you ask how.

It's in the DNA. During his research a geneticist in 1993 suggested the existence of a gay gene. Other research has found that being gay or lesbian tends to run in families. A 2012 study proposed that epigenetic changes or alterations in marks on DNA that turn certain genes on and off may play a role in homosexuality. This type of gene regulation isn't as stable as DNA and can be switched on and off by environmental factors or conditions in the womb during parental development. How such gay genes get passed down from generation to generation has puzzled scientist. Does every gay person have this gene? In my opinion no but I believe it exists and the original gay gene creates and sets its on environment driven by the spirit that has found its kin. The spirit becomes a fertilizing agent as it grows and develops causing a full lifestyle with aggressive passion, extreme energy and intelligence. Driven by the combination of the gene and spirit it becomes powerful and you can feel the spirit of this influence because this powerful spirit draws like a magnet through personality and is opened to those that appear to be different or alienated as it creates its own communities by seeking a place of comfort and acceptability. As the spirit seeks to find a home it embraces and develops an appetite for this lifestyle which becomes rewarding for them in their community and place of acceptance. The bible says in Matthew 12:23, "When the unclean spirit is gone out of a man, he walketh through dry places, seeking rest," Spirits are always looking for a place to dwell. They start out by hanging around looking for opportunities to influence you which leads to oppression. At this point I believe the gene begins to wake up. Spirits seek out their own kind so they can have a comfortable environment for free expression because some are more wicked and stronger than others. This explains the erotic appetite of man's corruption. Through these corrupt genes Satan has enrolls to man's character and behavior. This explains why man would desire a man over a beautiful woman and woman desires a woman over a handsome man, which is against the natural nature. Romans 1:26-27, says "For this cause God gave them up unto veil affections: for even their woman did change the natural use into that which is against nature: And likewise also the man, leaving the natural use of a woman, burn in their lust one towards another; men with men working that which is unseemly, and receiving in themselves that recompense of their error which was meet." Let's look at Sodom and Gomorrah. When the angels of the Lord came to Lot's home the mob saw them enter and came to Lot's door requesting that they come out so they may know them. Instead Lot offered his virgin daughters who were beautiful but their desire wasn't for a woman. The men desired the two male angels. Through Sodom and Gomorrah we have an example of this dominate perverted spirit and how each generation has to deal with it because it's in the natural DNA and according to this theory the spiritual DNA as well. You might ask the question how, how does this gene wake up? Because demonic spirits never die they oppress, possess and influence. If bees know there is sugar inside they will swarm around and find a way in if at all possible. Based on this Satan has set up his kingdom in man from the very beginning. How? By separating man from God and introducing this tainted and perverted DNA. This is something that we're just coming around to in our understanding now that we've become more advanced in technology. Through genealogy we can now trace the heritage in our blood to see the percentages of the make up in our DNA whether it is 40% Black, 10% Indian, 15% European, 34% Asian or .5% unknown. What is the unknown? What type of sin runs through your family? Do you have thieves, liars and whoremongers? This gives a new understanding of blood and how everything is based on blood, especially the atoning. Now that man has become infected with the evil DNA from the fallen angels which caused man to become sinful. We now have a greater understanding of why God set up blood sacrifices in order for man to come before him. Hebrews 10:5-9, says, "Wherefore when he cometh into the world, he saith, sacrifice and offerings thou wouldest not, but a body has thou prepared me: and burnt offerings and sacrifices for sin thou has had no pleasure. Then said I, lo, I come in the volume of the book it is written of me, to do thy will, oh God. Above when he said, sacrifice and offering and burnt offerings and offerings for sin thou wouldest not, neither hadst pleasure therein; which are offered by the law; then said he, I come to do thy will, O God. He taketh away the first, that he may establish the second." God's sacrifices had to be performed a certain way depending on the level of sin but the corruption of sin in man had become so repetitive it caused a blood bath of innocent animals to be sacrificed. God so loved man, his creation he didn't leave him without a way out. After all this fight started in heaven and came to man, which caused blood to be spilled. The DNA had to hit the ground because Satan changed realms coming out the spirit into the natural. (How could man deal with that he's only human) You see Satan was playing the long game but

God seeing the long game, set a plan in place himself by hiding the power in the flesh of woman by way of Jesus. This is all about blood. Man needed a blood transfusion, a cleansing of 100% pure stock untainted blood, not touched by man or Satan but only by the hand of God. For without the shedding of blood there is no remission of sin. So the spiritual realm was once again transformed through the same way Satan infected man, except the DNA had to remain 100% pure. So the Holy Ghost impregnated Mary to give birth to the pure blood of God in the flesh from the spiritual realm into the natural realm. God being masterful played the game better and Jesus was born to redeem man back to God. Now this was the game changer and the battle that was in heaven is now here on earth, the only difference is, man is in the middle and the war between Christ and Satan commenced. If Satan could've tainted Christ like he tainted man he would've won but Christ is the champion of man, the hope of glory and didn't allow himself to be tainted like man did. Instead Satan fell into Gods trap. The moment he crucified Jesus, he let the untainted pure blood of God in the flesh hit the ground, bringing both realms together because Christ came through woman, walked amongst man without sin, showing man the way of victory by taking back the keys to death hell and the grave. This gets deep. Jesus was on the cross and a thief was there. The thief accepted Christ and made it into heaven but where did he leave his DNA? Could there have been a son or daughter that carried the gene? Could this be why some people are just natural born thieves? If the gene is passed on through generations, then the spirit is waiting for its home to mold and cultivate. God didn't leave man without an out and through confession in the spirit and accepting Jesus Christ as your Lord and Savior you become born again, cleansed through the blood of Jesus Christ, which allows man to escape his tainted sinful nature. So it doesn't matter if you're a homosexual, a thief, a liar or a whoremonger. God didn't leave us in the mess; he sent his best, so you have no excuse! God is caring and very powerful; he is also a God of war and has never lost a battle. You must understand this fight has three levels, psychological, spiritual and physical because everything starts in the mind. If you get the mind, you can break someone's spirit, if you can break their spirit, you can oppress them into doing something in the flesh that's against the will of God. In battle the enemy always looks for the weakest place to strike and in most cases it's the woman. This is what happened to Adam. Satan got to eve who was the weaker vessel and used her to get into Adams mind which caused him to disobey God. Even Samson said they tampered with my woman. You see Samson told a riddle nobody knew but him. He gave them seven days to figure it out or they would have to pay up. So what they did was threaten his wife by saying they'd burn her father's house down. Does this technique sound familiar? They got in her mind and for seven days she cried, causing her to get into the mind of Samson, until it broke his spirit, which lead him to tell his wife the answer to the riddle. She told them the answer to the riddle at the end of the seventh day and when they gave Samson the answer he said these words. "If you had not plowed with my heifer, ye had not found out my riddle." Then it went to the flesh and got physical. Samson went down to Ashkelon and slew thirty men all because they got in the mind of the woman; she got in mind of her man and broke his spirit. He got angry and physical and as a result thirty men died all because of a bet. Please understand this was introduced by Satan in the garden and this is what you're up against every day. God has your back you must trust in him no matter how thin the ice is that you're standing on. Psychological, spiritual and physical warfare, this is the game and the rules were set before you were born. Jacob was who he was before he was born and this was the same for Esau, as well as the same for you. So are you the Man on the Goat Trail or the Man in the Safari Suit? DNA is the hereditary material that makes up all human beings; it's the genetic makeup in all human cells which travel from generation to generation. Yes, natural DNA. So we now understand that kissing someone or exchanging bodily fluids can be dangerous because you don't know the genetics of the other persons DNA. Some say they're four generations inside a person's genetic makeup if not more. When you come in contact with someone you're coming in contact with their mother and father, their mother and father's mother and father, plus four other generations and whatever they've picked up along the course of their life. Exchanging breath is exchanging spirits because spirits move on breath. If you exchange any type of bodily fluids with someone who has a disease, illness etc. you ingest their DNA. Whoever you kiss can pass an evil spirit and you won't understand why you start acting a certain way. The exchanging of bodily fluids is serious. Take a married couple for instance, the bible says they become one flesh. Let's look at becoming one. When a married couple kisses they exchange body fluids and when they have sex they exchange bodily fluids. When he says she is mine and I am hers its true, his DNA is running through her body and her DNA is running through his body. Their spirits become common with one another to the point where she can feel him and he can feel her. If their faith and belief is on one accord it creates a power that only a couple can produce by their spirits and faith. This is the chemistry that makes a powerful force. The longer they're together the stronger they become. The aura of these two will demand their space to the lesser. This is why some couples began to act and look alike after years of being together. She can tell what he is going to say or if he's lying, he can be in the store she can think it and he is lead to bring it. This is why you seek to find a soul mate or someone you can share your life with. That's why it's imperative to be on one accord and not allow any breech between what you have, which is special. If you're married and you kiss someone else you create a breech. If you have sex with someone else you create a breech which causes your spirit to change because you've been infected with someone else's DNA and body fluid. Now their spirit has passed into yours by way of breath and has now massaged into your spirit causing changes in your emotions and your partner can feel this change. The connection has been interrupted because your passion has been elevated and it now shows through your walk, talk and aura. Some say you're glowing. You're countenance reflects the adrenaline rush that heated the blood running through your body. This changed your eyes because they were getting dim and now you see brightness due to being excited again. The freshness of your skin changes as you now buy a new perfume/cologne and sporting a different hair style. You're no longer settled but right and ready like you were when you first meet your spouse; this is why you must keep the life in your marriage so it won't slip away before your very own eyes. You must not allow bills and the struggle of life to kill what was once the best thing that ever happened to you. You must also be aware of your children being blockers because children will bring problems to your happy home creating chaos within your marriage. From me to you don't allow time and trials to become your embrace; the coat you wear into the death of your relationship. As I speak to you through the reading of my words. Go get a new hair style and fragrance and do something fun with your spouse to make yourself laugh because you know what you have but you don't know what you'll get. The character of a person in my opinion is molded by their genetic makeup along with their spiritual and natural upbringing. Families have spirits that have attached themselves, some call it generational curses. These are no more than demonic spirits which one of your ancestors may have made a pact with and that spirit has become common in the breeding of your family. Let's look at a biblical character named Gomer. Gomer became a victim of her ancestry and the evil DNA was in her blood, this was her breed; Gomer inherited these immoral tendencies which later manifested themselves. Gomer was a woman of harlotry; she was a product of her environment because it was in her genes. Gomer's character was molded by the spirit that dwelled in her surroundings causing Gomer to be deprived because of her ancestry and the evil taint flowing in her blood. Gomers mother also engaged in the profession so the apple didn't fall far from the tree. Can you imagine living the life of a whore? Can you imagine coming up hearing people talk about your mother and the things she did to make her money? This must have had an effect on Gomer, hearing all the slander and gossip which cultivated the spirit within her. Gomer's mother was a whore and Gomer became a whore, this was the spirit she embraced. It became her lifestyle; this is what Gomer grow up in. As she watched her mother and listened to the things her mother would say along with other woman in her community. As a result Gomer developed a resistance to criticism by other woman. The bible speaks in Proverbs 2:16, "to deliver thee from the strange woman, even from the stranger which flattereth with her words;" The bible also says in Proverbs 7: 15-18, "therefore came I forth to meet thee, diligently to seek thy face, and I have found thee. I have decked my bed with coverings of tapestry, with carved works, with fine linen of Egypt. I have perfumed my bed with myrrh, aloes, and cinnamon. Come let us take our feel of love until the morning: Let us solance ourselves with loves." Wow! The bible is so powerful with truth. Can you imagine the DNA flowing through this woman? Did you know that when you engage with someone through kissing you exchange saliva? In that saliva lies thirty people for every one person you kissed or exchanged body fluids with. Let's take a look at ST. Luke 8:2, "And certain woman, which had been healed of evil spirits and infirmities, Mary called Magdalene, out of whom went seven devils," This type of woman always has a lot going on within her. Spirits are invisible and breath is invisible. So when you kiss someone not only are you sharing DNA, there's also a transference of spirits taking place. Yes. You kissed someone and now you're wondering why you're acting differently. Your passion has become more enhanced, you're lusting more and you've become a little wilder. All because you had a DNA injection and caught a new spirit. Now let's take a look at Rahab she was referred to as a harlot several times in the bible. In the book of Joshua 2:1, "An Joshua the son of Nun sent out of Shittim two men to spy secretly, saying, go view the land, even Jericho. And they went, and came into a harlot's house, named Rahab, and lodged there." This lets me know that Rahab had a very nice establishment equipped with an upstairs and downstairs for eating, drinking, lodging and pleasure if desired. Rahab was a business woman who was well established. She was a real entrepreneur and a woman of opportunity who yielded herself by using what she had to get what she needed. Rahab was influenced by the spirit of need; as she entertained and developed her reputation of holding, sharing and selling secret information. Rahab knew things that most people would never know because she had a full service operation which created an atmosphere for spirits to dwell because travelers always talk and gossip is always moving. So merchants and traveling men came to Rahab's place not just for pleasure but for counsel and information as well. The bible speaks of the two spies that Joshua sent; they came to Rahab's place. "Rahab seeing the two men were men of God helped them" This is how Rahab found out about Joshua's plan. When Rahab discerned it was real she understood that life as she knew it was now over. Rahab saw an opportunity to jump ship because the one she was on was going to sink. Let me pause here. There comes a time when people must realize that nothing is forever and change will take place because time brings about a change. So either you move with the move or be ran over by the move. In this case Rahab moved with the move and ended up brokering a deal for her and her family. Yes. You can make the right move and save your family but you must be willing to move when you see the hand of God. Too many of us are stubborn and think we have more time and lose in the end. The will of God is beyond where you are, even now. Rahab had to make a drastic change that required believing and having faith, that if she did the right thing, God would bless her and God did. Rahab ended up marrying one of the men of God named Salmon, who was one of the spies. As a result, Rahab gave birth to Boaz, who married Ruth, which led to Obed, which lead to Jesse, who fathered David, through whose blood line Jesus was born, in whom Mary was the host, as we all know.

CHAPTER 2

UNRAVELING

The bible says in Psalms 51:5, "Behold, I was shapen in iniquity; and in sin did my mother conceive me." Gomer was born into an unholy lifestyle; it was in her genes as she was shaped in iniquity. This was the spirit of Gomer's home and when that gene got a full healthy development, it mimicked its environment because just like anything else, for good growth it has to be cultivated and the ground must be good. (In this case I'm talking about spiritual influence) Most people are victims of their environment. This is why you must be aware of your children's environment and careful of whom you allow your children to go around. Why would you allow your babies to go around uncle beer and auntie smoke and you know they have bad spirits? You must protect your children because spirits travel through breathe and when uncle beer and auntie smoke kiss them in the mouth a transference of spirits takes place and you're now wondering why little wookie has started to act funny. So it's important to pray and anoint your children. Let's go back to Gomer. God chose to put a holy with an unholy. Hosea

1:2, says "And the Lord said to Hosea, go, take unto thee a wife of whoredoms and children of whoredoms:" God has a reason for everything and his power is absolute. So there is no way evil can win as long as you obey God. The bible states in 1 Corinthians 7:14, "For the unbelieving husband is sanctified by the wife, and the unbelieving wife is sanctified by the husband: else were your children unclean: but now are they holy." The problem is people start disobeying God by stepping outside the boundaries and doing things their own way. As they play russian-roulette with heaven and hell because they have no fear of God. Just like a mouse playing with a trap that has a big piece of cheese on it. The mouse doesn't have the patience to wait until someone drops a crumb on the floor. Just like some of you, who can't wait on God to provide? For some have lost hope in the miracles God has promised them and they have grown weary. Your faith shouldn't be like trying to hold on to a slippery fish, you should have a firm grip. So no matter what life throws your way, you must hold to the faith that was delivered to you. Romans 8:24-25, says "For we are saved by hope: but hope that is seen is not hope: for what a man seeth, why doth he yet hope for it? But if we hope for that we see not, then do we with patience wait for it." So in our patience we gain experience; and experience hope. You must have faith in the power of God and work the plan he's given you. I imagine Hosea must have said to himself a whore because he was a holy man and she was an unholy woman; unclean, full of spirits and other men's DNA. Gomer's mind had to be moving so fast that she couldn't hear nor listen but God and his power can change a mind and drive out evil spirits, causing a person to have peace.

Hosea allowed himself to be used by God, just like you must allow yourself to be used of God and trust the God in your life. You must have patience, pray for them and allow the process to work. Don't give up so easily, ask how can I help? Sometimes it's the little things. Like showing them that you care by inviting them to your church or your family barbeque so they can see true Christian fellowship with fun and games without worldly music and foul language. Now that's being a vessel that God can use to inspire someone. You must understand it takes time for some people to get delivered and quit as it's kept; you're not totally delivered yourself. You still got some stuff going on in your life, yet you're still working in his kingdom. So don't pass judgment on someone else who's struggling. God always chooses to use a vessel and in Gomer's case it was Hosea. The power of God was with Hosea so Hosea detoxed Gomer with his presence, his spirit, his DNA, his environment and the Holy Spirit that dwelled within him. Through this Gomer was sanctified by communion with the man of God. Do you know the power of love is the greatest force that erases sin? But you must allow time to have its full work. It wasn't easy for Hosea but Hosea was determined to obey God. Gomer is a prime example that sometimes you have to get them back. This is a soul that has to be unraveled. So don't let the devil have them, put some work in and don't give up or be lazy. It's just like that jump rope that was all tangled up when you were a little girl but you unraveled it little by little. So keep fighting I promise you will win if you don't give in. (Some may not agree with me and say I'm off, but that's ok keep living) Now Rahab I truly believe was a business woman who embraced her environment. The spirits around

Rahab were strong and these demons had a grip on her as she yielded herself because she had no option. This is why it's good to witness and present people with an option; a choice to stay in bondage or seek to be set free by the power of God. When Rahab's opportunity presented itself, Rahab chose to believe the two men of God and her faith changed her path. Rahab wasn't afraid to change direction; sometimes your deliverance is in changing direction, as you follow your heart and not the influence of people. People will tell you God didn't say that or I don't believe that's the will of God for your life. Some leaders will even go as far as saying you're not going to be blessed. I say to you if it's not sin and you're not doing something in defilement, then follow the God in your life. How can they know what God is telling you? The bible says in Philippians 2:12, "Wherefore, my beloved, as ye have always obeyed, not as in my presence only, but now much more in my absence, work out your own salvation with fear and trembling." Change is never easy and people will hold you for their own benefit. So don't be afraid to step out on faith. Rahab wasn't. She gave up everything and her gift made room for her. As she married Salmon, one of the two spies she helped. Yes. Rahab found the love of her life; talking about opportunity, Rahab was blessed big time and because she believed, she became the mother of Boaz and he married Ruth that led to Jesse the father of David whose blood line Jesus was born. Just think about this for a moment. Rahab the harlot had a blood line of kings. Rahabs story is a prime example of believing because you never know what God has for you, if you can only believe all things are possible. The bible tells us in Proverbs 3:5, "Trust in the Lord with all thine heart; and lean not unto thine own understanding." Wow. What an unravelling. Demonic spirits have a lot of people bound. So your job is to seek the Lord in how he wants to use you but first you must be spiritual enough to know that evil is real, alive and on its job day and night. Ask yourself who are you helping to get unraveled from evil spirits? Or are you yourself bound by some? Sometimes people get caught up with the wrong people, without understanding that everyone has their own spirit. Man is made up of body, soul and spirit. Genesis 2:7, says "And the Lord God formed man of the dust of the ground, and breathed into his nostrils the breathe of life; and man became a living soul." Genesis 1:26-27, says "And God said, Let us make man in our image, after our likeness: and let them have dominion over fish of the sea, and over the fowl of the air, and over the cattle, and over all the earth, and over every creeping thing that creepeth upon earth. So God created man in his own image, in the image of God created he him; male and female created he them." Man is Gods masterpiece and God seen it was not good for man to be alone. So if you read the first three chapters of Genesis you see God placed man in the Garden of Eden with his wife Eve. God enjoys fellowship because there's fellowship in heaven. Notice how God speaks in Genesis 1:26, "God said, Let us make man in our image, after our likeness:" I don't know about you but if I'm talking like the scripture reads, I'm talking to someone in my presence. The bible says in 1 John 5:7-8, "For there are three that bare record in heaven, the Father, the Word and the Holy Ghost: and these three are one. And there are three that bare witness in earth, the spirit, and the water, and the blood: and these three agree in one." But you can't forget about Satan, the fallen angels along with his host of demons. Satan was watching everything God did and he wanted everything God had. It was Satan's jealousy, envy and rebellion that got him kicked out of heaven. Is that you? Are you a liar, jealous, envious, rebellious, unforgiven, full of wrath etc.? If so stop! God intended for mans temple to be his dwelling place, so his spirit can commune with the human spirit and the spirit and soul would use the body as a means of expression. Here spirit and soul being the puppeteer and the body being the puppet. In my opinion the soul comes into the world pure in its infant state with the spark of life only God can give. The body also contains blood, tissue, organs and DNA but because man has a free will. Paul said in 1 Corinthians 9:17, "If I do these things willingly, I have a reward:" Understand free will is hard because the soul has been seduced, led captive, darkened and poisoned with self-interest. This is what happened to Eve because of her own self-interest she allowed herself to be seduced by Satan, who is the master of seduction and then she seduced her husband Adam. Notice what the bible says in Romans 5:19, "For as by one man's disobedience many were made sinners," The command was given to Adam, he was the head but Eve seduced him. (Satan has always used a woman to seduce man) God enjoyed his walk with his masterpiece but the fellowship was fractured; there was a breech because evil penetrated man and got between the fellowship of God and his masterpiece. Here's the pattern of how it works. Evil influences steal the soul of man from God. Just like Satan influenced one third of the angels in heaven to follow him. These evil spirits know how to influence you and trap you. That's why you must be careful of your fellowship; just like some have entertained angels, some have also entertained demons. The character of man is molded by spirits, so your upbringing is important. Some people have darker souls. Their character is charismatic and compelling, causing one to gravitate to them because they are worldly and enjoy the freedom to say, do and act the way they want to. Satan knows money is a powerful source because you desire to have more and more. Take a young lady for example. A man pulls up in a luxury car; he's tall, handsome, well-groomed, smelling good and dressed from head to toe. Though he's charming, he's the devil looking for prey and when he approaches the young lady she's in trouble. Most women are looking for a good man to satisfy their need for love and security. So they let their guard down and become used, which leads to heart break, causing some woman to become bitter. After one or two experiences like this a woman becomes angry, unable to trust and hate sets in. This begins a cycle of permissive behavior that only the power of God can deliver her from. Believe it or not the evil spirit are watching and have now influenced her children as they take on this lifestyle, by mimicking their mother. Could you be auntie Smoke? Who stopped looking for love and became a love vessel? You see it was all about the money to auntie Smoke, as she makes her on security and drives her own luxury car. This is how auntie Smoke mends her spirit but she doesn't realize she's on her way to hell. Which was Satan's plain from the beginning and it all started from one word. Desire. Desire meaning to want or wish for something: to feel for something: to want to have sex with someone: to express a wish for something: impulse towards something, longing, craving, sexual urge or appetite. Did you know spirits are eternal? Yes. Spirits are eternal and they aren't in a hurry because time is on their side and they have watched you sense your childhood to gain more and more influence over your life. These evil spirits have associates the bible states in St. Luke 11:26, "Then goeth he, and taketh to him seven other spirits more wicked them himself; and they enter in, and dwell there: and the last state of that man is worse than the first." Wow! Eve desired the forbidden fruit and auntie Smoke desired the man in the luxury car. Your desires must be controlled. You're probably now thinking, how can you control your desires? The answer is through the power of God. God tries to help you but God knows something's must run their course because most of you aren't interested in what God is offering because it requires changing your life. Most people have strong desires and Satan feeds that desire. Satan will meet the need and continue to massage your soul with one of his lures, music. The bible says in Ezekiel 28:13-15, "Thou has been in Eden the garden of God; every precious stone was thy covering, the sardius, topaz, and the diamonds, the beryl, the onyx, and the jasper, the sapphire, the emerald, and the carbuncle, and gold: the workmanship of thy tabrets and of thy pipes was prepared in thee in the day that thou was created. Thou art the anointed cherub that covereth; and I have set thee so: thou was upon the holy mountain of God; thou has walked up and down in the mist of stones and fire. Thou was perfect in thy ways from the day thou was created, till iniquity was found in thee." So this tells you Satan was created for worship and certainly has musical abilities. Isaiah 14:11, says "Thy pomp is brought down to the grave, and the noise of the viols:" Lucifer was created as an organic organ; he was a living musical instrument. The world system uses music to seduce, corrupt and gain riches, so they can have power. In the world we all know money is power, so you become hooked by beats and lyrics which captivate you. Music will draw you in or drive you out. Did you know spirits can be controlled by music, as well as possess and influence you through music? Do you know subliminal messages are in some music? Yes, evil chants are hidden in some music which is satanically inspired. Many have died and went to hell listening to and serving these evil spirits. The spirit behind the music carries over when you play it in your home it will change the mood and you know I'm right. Truth be told. If you haven't been saved all your life you can give the artist name and title to the song you made your first child on. Some music carries seducing spirits. The lyrics are designed that way because the artist is controlled, inspired and anointed by demons that move on them and some are even possessed. You better listen to me, the beats and words in some music are so strong you find yourself singing it in your mind two days later. You can hear a song that will bring back memories, taking you back to your first time or a bad experience. This is why I don't listen to worldly music; gospel music is it for me. Take a moment and think about your family; think about the family barbeque. You know uncle flat foot gone play his down home music and auntie butterscotch gone do her dance, with her drink in her hand. So when you Christians go to the family barbeque say hello, get your plate and move on. Don't go and spoil the barbeque because there's always those confessing but not possessing. Truth be told they can't let their hair down until you leave, especially those who supposed to have some God. Yet they're getting their head bad with some of the wicked juice aunt butterscotch got behind her bar. While sitting at the card table just waiting on the bid wiz game to get started and trust me they not playing to pass time. After you leave the barbeque, get in your car, turn your gospel music up, detox and thank God for your deliverance. Did you know anointed music drives out certain demons? When music is played by a skilled anointed musician the power of God comes through because God controls all spirits. The bible says in 1 Samuel 16:23, "And it came to pass, when the evil spirit from God was upon Saul, that David took a harp, and played with his hand: so Saul was refreshed, and was well, and the evil spirit departed from him." Did you know you can be spiritually sick? The bible said Saul was refreshed. Meaning to be restored, strengthened or replenished. Also the bible said Saul was well. When you have a broken spirit from bad news, someone hurting your feelings or you've become overwhelmed because of your circumstances, music puts you in a certain mood. When a good praise and worship song comes on your hands go up in the air and tears start rolling down your face because deliverance has come. This is why the minister of music is so important when you go to the house of God. His job is to stand at the gate and make sure the songs, tones and music is of God and not inspired by demons. So this person must be full of the Holy Ghost with a burning fire and anointed of God because the yolk shall be destroyed because of the anointing. When you have the music right it starts the spiritual washing. You've been going all week fighting evil spirits on your job and in the streets. So when you come to the house of God your soul needs a washing and the music soaks you real good. So when the

Man of God brings the word of God you receive a charge, you're refreshed and you break through ready for the next week. That's why the house of God must have its own sound; we must keep it pure and true to God. Each generation has its own battle of new sounds and new instruments. Dear ministers of music and musicians of God listen to me; you must hold the line and not let the devil come in the house of God. You must seek God for a new sound from heaven not the cords of worldly music. How can the world come up with new songs inspired by demons and you can't come up with new songs inspired by God, yet you say you have the spirit of God? Every generation has its own outlook on music and you have your challenge, which is to protect the front line. We're looking to the God in your life because you're our modern day David. Be true to your call, it's always been easy to copy off of someone else's paper but if you do the work yourself, then you know it's right. Remember heaven is listening to you, so it's time to get busy. The church is getting worldly and being diluted by Satan's kingdom through social pressure and the restructuring of the church. Satan's kingdom is set up to weaken and confuse the church. Satan realizes the church can't be stopped, so his strategy is to infiltrate the church with worldliness. The economic system makes it hard for a righteous man and woman of the kingdom to survive. This is why you must seek to work in Gods kingdom and support one another. The bible says in Ephesians 6:12, "For we wrestle not against flesh and blood, but against principalities, against powers, against the rulers of darkness of this world, against spiritual wickedness in high places." We must understand there different kinds of demons and different levels of wickedness in high places;

they might be invisible to your naked eye but trust me, they're just as real as natural creatures. The music industry is full of wealth, riches, fame and lots of fortune. So the temptation has now become musical beats that you can step to in the night club and shout to in the church because the beat was inspired by demons and not by the Holy Spirit. Substituting lyrics like he or him instead of using the name Jesus. Talking about I'm in love with him. Him who? You see it's all about the money. Gospel music has finally gone main stream, the more worldly it sounds the more lucrative it is. The church has taken down because their trying to reach the youth. Yes the church has lowered the standards all because they're trying to reach the youth. I'm not saying not to reach the youth but when I got saved being saved wasn't popular either. I had to give up my jazz collection, all my blues, my R&B, drinking, smoking and my girlfriends to. The bible says in 2 Corinthians 5:17, "Therefore if any man be in Christ, he is a new creature: old things are passed away; behold, all things are become new." This is a privilege, that every born again man or woman receive the spirit of sonship and seek God for the fullness of his spirit. We're like modern day holy men and woman chosen to serve God. The bible says in ST. Luke 16:13, "No servant can serve two masters: for either he will hate the one, and love the other; or else he will hold to the one, and despise the other. Ye cannot serve God and mammon." You see gospel artist are gifted by God and anointed but demons watch them and report back to Satan and pressure is put on them because they desire fame, fortune, money and the prestige of lights, camera, action, which will cause them to backslide. So the artist is an artist who wants to cross over into the world so they make their music sound worldly, get the money and still label it gospel music. (I meant to say modern day gospel) You see the church has wanted to be accepted by the world so bad that they've lowered the standard. So people of the world feel comfortable walking into Gods house half dressed, as they listen to this modern day music, that doesn't bring conviction because it sounds like the same music they dance to in the night club. So there's no power to drive out demons because the demon is singing, flaming and directing. No Holy Ghost anywhere as the church is being bamboozled, bewitched and bound.

CHAPTER 3

BORN AGAIN

Genesis 2:22, says "And the rib, which the Lord God had taken from man, made he a woman, and brought her unto the man." God created woman for man. So this scripture tells us that there's a woman for every man. Love is power; love produces a strong emotion that creates passion which leads to love making. So when a man is with a woman he's in sync. We all know when a man and a woman have sexual intercourse (make love) they exchange body fluids. When the man ejaculates into the woman there're five hundred little fertilizing agents looking for the egg of the woman. At the point of contact there's a charge of life and in that moment a soul is created. This is the miracle of creation, as the embryo is nurtured and begins its development so it can become healthy and strong. Think about it for a moment. Five hundred sperm cells were trying to get in that egg but only one made it. This is the natural process of life but there's a spiritual process as well. Jesus told Nicodemus in ST. John 3:3, "verily, verily, I say unto thee, Except a man be born again, he cannot see the kingdom of God," Notice in verse 6, "That which is born of flesh is flesh: And that which is born of the spirit is spirit." Nicodemus was thinking from the natural but Jesus was speaking from the spiritual. New life in the spirit is a process. This brings to mind the scripture in ST. Luke 13:24, "Strive to enter in at the straight gate: For many, I say unto you, will seek to enter in, and shall not be able." Which brings me to another scripture ST. Matthew 7:14, "Because straight and narrow is the way, which leadeth unto life, and few there be that find it." It's a miracle within itself to be able to get past the world with all its lust, deceit and entanglements. Along with family and friends who don't understand when you begin to seek out the true and living God. Which requires leaving the crowd and all you're familiar with as you race forward to make a connection and become charged by the spirit of God as you birth into a new world, called the kingdom of God. The bible says in 2 Corinthians 5:17, "Therefore if any man be in Christ, he is a new a creature: old things are passed away; behold, All things are become new." You must be born again. The bible states in 1 Peter 1:23, "Being born again, not of corruptible seed, but of incorruptible, by the word of God which liveth and abideth forever." Jesus is the living Word and the bible tells us that in the beginning was the Word. The first chapter of the book of St. John lays out some serious facts about the Word. The bible states in St. John 1:3-4, "All things were made by him: and without him was not anything made that was made. In him was life; and the life was the light of men." The bible says in St. John 1:1, "In the beginning was the Word, and the Word was with God, and the Word was God." For we all know God spoke the world into existence through the Word and then God formed man of the dust of the ground and breathed into his nostrils the breathe of life: and man became a living soul. Man was made pure in his heart but Satan knew how to deal with matters concerning the heart and injected deceit. Satan deceived Eve who was the weaker vessel which caused her to yield to his influence, as Satan worked through her to influence Adam because he knew she was the key to Adams heart. Adam and Eve were caught in the deceitful plan of Satan in which his only goal was to take something from God. Remember Satan already influenced a third of heaven and now he had done the same to Adam and Eve. God cast Satan out of heaven and as a result of Adam and Eve disobedience God cast them out of the Garden of Eden. The bible states in Genesis 3:22 "And the Lord God said, behold, the man is become as one of us, to know good and evil: and now, lest he put forth his hand, and take also of the tree of life, and eat, and live forever:" So God put an angel by the tree of eternal life so sin wouldn't be eternal. I heard a preacher say "We have Gods blood because he created us so we will always be saved." When I heard that I said Lord help him, he has it wrong. We all know God will have no part of sin because the bible tells us that disobedience is as the sin of witchcraft and it also says when sin is finished, it brings forth death. Now that man was kicked out of the Garden of Eden there was no ark of safety for him. The bible says in Romans 5:19, "By one man's disobedience many were made sinners." Now if the bible says ten thousand, times ten thousand and thousands of thousands, a third part of that, are a lot of evil fallen angels. Who're just waiting for their chance to do the same thing Satan did or worse. (So Satan was just the beginning of man's sorrows) Fallen angels are capable of operating in the spiritual realm and the earthly realm. Angels have done and can do all things that man can do, plus things that man can't do because they're immortals who can appear and disappear. The bible says in Genesis 6:2, "That the sons of God saw the daughters of man that they were fair; and they took them wives of all which they chose." When the sons of God came unto the daughters of man and they bared children to them, God saw that the wickedness of man was great. (Now this is a lot of evil DNA being passed through bodily fluids). These evil spirits were perverted in their sexual nature; they had unnatural sex with man. I believe DNA is passed on and on and some lay dormant. Some will not agree with me but things runs through the DNA of your blood. I believe this same eternal evil can sniff out as it waits for the manifestation of that character or gene, so it can find a home to live within and influence. You must understand these spirits never die because they're eternal and they thrive in communities like Sodom and Gomorrah. Now we're living in a modern day Sodom and Gomorrah. This type of lifestyle creates social pressure that becomes powerful, creative, wealthy and full of energy. This lifestyle has become a magnet which is so powerful that no one can control it because these demonic spirits have the experience of time on their side. That's why you must obey the will of God and have faith in what he has laid out for you to follow because God has and always will send deliverance for his people. You must understand God will not twist your arm; you must be willing to trust and obey. God saw the mess man had put himself in, so the living Word decided to give man an out but it would require faith and obedience to the will of God. So by the obedience of one shall many be made righteous? God designed a plan to make the Word flesh which would allow man to receive eternal life. The bible states in St. John 1:14, "And the Word was made flesh, and dwelled amongst us, (and we beheld his glory, the glory as of the only begotten of the father,) full of grace and truth." God pulled a fast one on Satan, who had no idea he was about to lose again, but this time forever. The key was to shed the incorruptible blood because without the shedding of blood there is no remission of sin. When Jesus our Lord died on the cross, his sacrifice gave us a way back to God. The bible states in ST. John 1:12-13, "But as many as received him, to them gave he power to become the sons of God, even to them that believed on his name: Which were born, not of blood, nor of the will of the flesh, nor of the will of man, but of God." You read the bible so you know what happened to Adam but now it's off Adam and on you. So you have no excuse if you confess with your mouth and believe with your heart that Jesus is Lord. This goes back to the beginning where the Word spoke, let there be and it was. The Word spoke life. So now by the Word being in the flesh and shedding his blood; the connection is speaking and confessing your belief in Jesus which creates life and gives you the right to become the son of God. Hebrews 12:24-25, says "And to Jesus the mediator of the new covenant, and to the blood of sprinkling, that speaketh better things than of Abel. See that ye refuse not him that speaketh. For if they escaped not who refused him that spake on earth, much more shall not we escape, if we turn away from him that speaketh from heaven:" Jesus told his disciples to go tarry in Jerusalem and wait for the promise of the father. You see God wasn't finished, he knew man needed more than just his will to go up against Satan and his demons. So God sent the Comforter, the Spirit of Truth, the Holy Ghost and told them they would receive power, after the Holy Ghost comes upon them and they did. The bible said in Acts 2:2-4, "And suddenly there came a sound from heaven as of a rushing mighty wind, and it filled all the house where they were sitting. And there appeared unto them cloven tongues like as of fire, and it set up on each of them. And they were filled with the Holy Ghost, and began to speak with other tongues, as the spirit gave them utterance." I don't know about you but that sounds like power in the spirit to me. The only way you can fight Satan is with the power of the Holy Ghost, which gives you power. Paul asked them in Acts 19:2, "He said unto them, have you received the Holy Ghost since ye believed? And they said unto him, we have not so much as heard whether there be any Holy Ghost." Now this is amazing because they're so many people in this same state of mind. The only difference is they've heard about the Holy Ghost but have not had the true experience of the power of the Holy Ghost. Notice what verse 6 says, "And when Paul had laid his hands upon them, the Holy Ghost came on them; And they spake with tongues, and prophesied." The reason why some of you don't get the Holy Ghost is because some men of God don't have it and don't want it in their church. This reminds me of the sons Sceva, who had seen the man of God cast out demons through the power of the Holy Ghost and thought they could do the same thing. Notice what the bible says in verse 14-16 "And there were seven sons of one Sceva, a Jew, and chief of the priests which did so. And the evil spirit answered and said, Jesus I know, And Paul I know; but who are ye? And the man in whom the evil spirit was leaped on them, and overcame them, and prevailed against them, so that they fled out of that house naked and wounded." Notice the bible says the chief priest was with them. Here the bible clearly reveals to you that some men of God don't have the Holy Ghost. This is why the bible tells you to know them that labor among you; you must be a man of God outside the church and not just when you come to church. This is why it's important to have a true personal experience with the power of the Holy Ghost, so when you come against a demonic force, you'll have the power to cast it out. Christ told Nicodemus you must be born again. Nicodemus asked can a man enter into his mother's womb twice? Jesus replied. That which is born of flesh, is flesh, that which is born of spirit, is spirit. In order to be born again you must be blood washed and cleansed by the blood of the lamb, Jesus Christ, the pure untainted blood. Remember you're tainted because the fallen angels infected man in the beginning with their evil DNA and now there's a process in getting back to God. Jesus gave instructions to his disciples to write down; these men were inspired by the Holy Ghost and given instructions by Jesus Christ, the son of the living God. It is written in the gospel and epistles of the bible on how to believe and receive. For the road map to heaven is clear and if you follow it, you will receive your deliverance. You'll have power to walk away from that alcohol bottle, power to put that cigarette, pipe, marijuana down, power to walk away from ungodly sex, power to stop stealing, lying and cheating. When you confess Christ and receive this power, the Holy Spirit will lead you in making decisions through the word and demons will have to back up. Once you're born again and receive the

Holy Ghost you can bind all those evil forces. Now that you've been redeemed back into the will of God you can help someone else to be set free. As you witness and tell your testimony of how God set you free from the hand of Satan and through the plan of salvation, you're justified and sanctified. Your eyes have now become open and you're just like a newborn baby. So now you see the world different because the scales are off your eyes, your heart is different, your walk and your talk is different, you have no desire to gamble, party or go clubbing, or be around anyone that's not talking about the goodness of God. Your nature has been changed; you have been washed by the blood of the lamb, the incorruptible seed. Now you need nourishment like any other baby does. So you begin to feed from the word of God to become strong in him, as you pray for guidance and to be led by his spirit because the world is no longer your friend, now that you've become a part of the kingdom of God. The bible says in 2 Corinthians 5:17, "Therefore if any man be in Christ, he is a new creature: old things are passed away; behold, all things are become new."

CHAPTER 4

MAINTAINING THE UNRAVELING

Spiritual DNA functions the same as natural DNA, formed by cells in the genetic makeup. The only difference is they're invisible, but none the less real. God gave each of us our own spirit. Hebrews 11:3, says "Through faith we understand that the worlds were framed by the word of God, so that things which are seen were not made of things which do appear." So this tells us the spiritual world is more powerful than the natural world and heavily populated. Think about all the people who've died since the beginning of time. Their bodies went back to the dirt, but their spirit and soul is eternal. Notice what Elisha said in 2nd Kings 6:16, 17 "And he answered, fear not: for they that be with us are more than they that be with them. And Elisha prayed, and said, Lord, I pray thee open his eyes, that he may see, and the Lord opened the eyes of the young man; and he saw: and behold, the mountain was full of horses and chariots of fire round about Elisha." So through the reading of this passage we understand the power of the spiritual realm. Allow me to use this analogy; they're good guys in the spirit, Gods gang so to speak but let's not forget the other gang, Satan's gang. Satanic forces are always trying to imprint on your spirit through influence which causes your character to become flawed but after you're born again and cleansed through the word of God, your nature is changed. So you must be careful not to be entangled again with the yoke of bondage. Look at what 2nd Peter 2:20, says "for if after they have escaped the pollution of the world through the knowledge of the Lord and Savior Jesus Christ, they are again entangled therein, and overcome, the latter end is worse with them than the beginning." So that being said, you must watch your choices now that you're free. Character is important. A person's spiritual DNA carriers a lot of scares, so when you choose a mate choose wisely.

Let's look at this chart for example

Blue Collar	White Collar
Country	City
Mechanics	Manager
Barber/Beautician	Lawyer
Maintenance/Custodian	Teacher/Educator
Streets	Suburbs
Tradesmen	Trader on Wall Street

Here we have different careers, different egos, different lifestyles and different spirits based on their life's journey and occupation. So let's take a look at Jacob and Esau spirit and how they interacted. God told Rebekah two nations are in thy womb and two manner of people. Isn't this amazing, two different spirits and characters coming from the same womb at the same time? (Talk about mixing up DNA) No two people have the same finger prints and no two people have the same eye retina; which is a layer at the back of the eye-ball containing cells that are unique in every person. Isn't God awesome? Jacob, the man in the safari suit was a smooth clean cut man, neat and orderly. He was an inside man. Esau, the man on the goat trail was a rugged cunning hunter. He was an outside man with long hair, a beard, wearing goat skin and smelling like the outside woods. Referring back to the chart, let's take a look at the difference between the city boy and the country boy. Here you have a man who grew up in a big city. (The concrete jungle) He's a city boy who grew up surrounded by tall buildings and paved streets. To see a bug was rare, unless it was a roach. The only animals he saw were dogs, cats and occasionally someone had a pet snake. It was normal for him to see the wine-head sitting at the bus stop and the prostitute standing outside the corner store. There were few trees to blow away the smell of urine and the stench coming from the garbage cans in the alley. He came up wearing slacks, shirts and dress shoes. He road public transportation and traffic was everywhere, as far as his eyes could see. Along with the loud sounds of the cab/car horns, police, ambulance and fire truck sirens coming from all four directions and let's not forget the pedestrians walking, joggers jogging, and cyclist cycling. If you walked through certain neighborhoods you had to be careful as you watched to avoid the gangs, which were everywhere. Along with the drug dealers, stickup man and drug addict. He had no father at home. Most of the time it was a man at home just not his real father. It amazes me how a man will leave his family and go be a father to someone else's children, all because of lust. Yes, that's a spirit. No one took him fishing, hunting or horseback riding. He didn't know anything about growing greens, peas and corn. He just went to the grocery store and bought whatever he needed. He didn't have chickens running around his backyard to feed off of, he bought all his meat from the meat market. He was an athlete; who played basketball from grammar school to high school. It was a recruiter who recommended he go to a small college in the south, so he could have a better opportunity and so he did. He took an Amtrak train that dropped him at a small train station in the woods. As he looked around all he saw was trees, a gravel road and the sounds of animals and bugs that he couldn't see, he could only hear them. Then he heard something coming down the road, it was a van the college sent to pick him up and boy o boy was he glad. This is how the city boy arrived in the country. What happens when the man in the safari suit, meets the woman on the goat trail? Or the man on the goat trail meets the woman in the safari suit? Will it work? Let's take a look at what happens when the city boy with a different spirit and lifestyle, meets the country girl whose spirit and life's journey is different. She's more of a home girl who's smart with mother's wit. She's a girl who's use to walking barefoot in the dirt. She can play with worms and snap a chicken's neck. She's seen the guts and smelled the blood of a fresh kill because she grew up with a father and brothers who taught her how to fish and use big fat worms called night crawlers as bait. She's held a shotgun and went hunting for deer, rabbit and squirrels. She's seen her father slaughter a hog as he skins it and keeps the intestines for chitterlings. She goes into the field and picks her greens, peas, tomatoes and pulls her corn fresh off the stalk. She's seen the guts flying when they're cleaning the fresh kill but here's a man that can't stand the sight of blood and will not touch guts. (They say opposites attract) She sees that city boy and likes that tall handsome clean cut man, who smells good and has sweet words. Can this couple make it? Are they good for one another? Somebody's going to be influenced and most likely the stronger spirit will over power the other. Somebody is going to slow down and adapt or somebody will speed up because of the rush. Let's change into a different flow for a minute. We're talking about maintaining and not being entangled with the yoke of bondage. Remember just because you can, don't mean you should. Different spirits, characters and lifestyles require sacrifice. Let's look at the husband mechanic; he's a blue collar and the wife who's a manager; she's a white collar. The mechanic deals in grease and has rough hands, as he crawls under cars and trucks to make his living. When he goes home his boots are oily, his clothes smell of musk, his fingers nails are dirty with grease and he's looking for his wife to wash his clothes and prepare his meal. You're a manager in a clean environment, you're well dressed, well-spoken and you don't like anything dirty. You know he makes good money and he's a good man and good men are hard to find but can you live together? Can you communicate? Because if you get entangled in this relationship it could end up in a divorce, so there must be some compromise. As we refer back to the chart, let's take a look at the tradesmen and the trader on Wall Street. Carpenters, plumbers and electricians make good money but money isn't everything. You trade on Wall Street but when you get home, what will you talk about? He has construction on his mind and you have stocks, bond and shares on yours. Can you make this work? I'm trying to get some of you to think before you jump. They're too many divorces and it becomes death to your relationship with God. Remember just because you can, don't mean you should! Did you know that lust is different from love? You must learn to sit down and count up the cost and evaluate if this relationship is good for your future. Let's look into the Barber/Beautician and the Lawyer. Now these occupations both deal with people that tell them their problems. The Barber/Beautician is one of the oldest trades. People talk while they're in the chair and the Barber/Beautician becomes a psychiatrist. They've heard so many stories that in some cases they have better advice and it's free. They work in a nice clean environment with music playing, which relaxes you as they make you look good. Now the Lawyer listens to people's problems as well but on a more serious note. Their time is money and they charge for their advice. Is this a couple that can get along? Or is the Lawyer more arrogant because they need more intellectual stimulation in their conversation when they get home because they bring their work home with them as well. Can this couple make it? Let's look at the suburbs and the city streets. The suburbs are quiet, the grass is well manicured, the yards are clean and they're no police cars with sirens racing through the streets. Families are home by a certain hour at night and the neighbors know one another. There're no gangs to worry about, they're living life at their own pace and they aren't use to drama. Now a person that comes up in the city streets is full of drama and use to drama. Their either in a gang or running from a gang, as they fight for everything they get. As they mark their territory and take on every challenge that comes their way, all because their ambitious and driven to have something in life. They're use to the noise of the city streets because ambulances, fire trucks, police cars and guns being fired, are the normal everyday noises, along with the fighting and arguing that goes on in most homes. My point is when you get saved it opens up a world that you normally wouldn't have excess to. The Kingdom of God has all type of people that come to Christ and when you meet in the house of God, now what you have in common is Jesus Christ. The bible tells us in 1 Thessalonians 5:12, "And we beseech you, brethren, to know them which labor among you, and are over you in the Lord, and admonish you;" If you take this part of the scripture at face value you need to know those whom you're in fellowship with. Paul also wrote in 3:5, "For this cause when I could no longer forbear, I sent to know your faith, lest by some means the tempter have tempted you, and our labor be in vain." You never would have meet the lawyer or the Wall Street trader, tradesmen, educator, mechanic, policeman, white collar worker, praising God, next to the blue collar worker. Amongst all the other different spirits, characters and souls that have been saved, whom are all trying to make it into glory. We sometimes get innocently bound. Just because opportunity presents itself, doesn't mean the devil didn't set it up. Yes, opposites do attract but this is when you should pause and say, is this a trick of the enemy or a gift from God. You must do your homework with the understanding that sometimes you're so heavenly minded, you're no earthly good. Yes, come out the spirit and check your flesh, remembering just because you can, doesn't mean you should. You must ask yourself, am I compatible with this person? What do we have in common, other than our belief? Because when you get home to relax and enjoy one another on all levels, you find out that you have a different conversation, your back ground is different, family is different, money is different, goals are different and all you have to enjoy is the sexual stimulation. Have you allowed yourself to get into a marriage out of lust and opportunity? (The devil is good at that) Was this your soul mate? Did you fast, pray and research? Yes, research. Did you ask the hard questions? Did you rebuke the flesh, bind the devil and ask God to open your eyes? This is your salvation and you don't want to get innocently bound because then you're bound for divorce. People have stuff in their family's blood line. You knew she liked men but what you didn't know was she liked women too and now you're in trouble and asking why? The answer is because you were lusting and looking at her hips. You saw how he was acting in the choir, but you married him anyway and now you want to fast and pray for God to fix it. Fix it Jesus, fix it, Jesus help me, Jesus, Jesus, Jesus is your cry. There two ways to believe God for something, before or after. Trust me believing God before is always better. Just because you get saved doesn't mean you stop using what life has taught you. You just convert your life experiences with you as an example and testament to the goodness of God and as a benefit for the kingdom, because wisdom is wisdom no matter where it comes from. That drunken unsaved uncle can give you the best advice that could save your life and a bunch of headaches, but you so spiritual you don't even want to speak to him. Don't be that way he needs your prayers, talk to him or her sometimes you just might win them to the Lord. Take these tips; they will carry you a long way. Nevertheless if you're in this battle, it can be won with a lot of give and take and Jesus, along with casting down all imagination and everything that exalt itself against the power of God, including past relationships and other relationships in your mind, spirit and DNA. You must cast them down and put it all under the blood or you will find yourself comparing your current spouse to your previous relationship along with the smells, words and sexual experiences. You must bind those thoughts and say loose here! For if they were so great, why didn't you marry them or stay with them? You must invest yourself and this takes denying your flesh, accepting them for who they are and not trying to make them something that they're not. Now that you've been wrestled out of the hand of the enemy and you're fully unraveled, you must maintain it. Salvation is free but there is an up keep and if you don't keep up with the word, you will find yourself back in the flesh entangled again because Satan has traps that he has strategically placed around you, even in the church. Have you ever heard of a false prophet? This is why you must know the word of God for yourself and look at your leader's life and make sure it lines up with the word of God and they're on the straight and narrow standing before God and not just preaching the word before the people, yet it stops when it hits their family.

Proverbs 16:25, says "There is a way that seemth right unto a man, but the end thereof are the ways of death." Proverbs 17:23, states "A wicked man taketh a gift out of the bosom to pervert the ways of judgment." Stay in the bosom of God and let him lead you in your heart, then you'll know what is right for your life. The bible says in Proverbs 3:5-6, "Trust in the Lord with all thine heart; and lean not unto thine own understanding. In all thy ways acknowledge him, and he shall direct thy paths." So don't allow anyone to take what God has given you in your heart, you see and feel the change and they do to, as well as the love. As you continue to live the life it means they have no escape and they know they must travel that very same road as well. So let no one vex your spirit Proverbs 17:22, says "A merry heart doeth good like a medicine: but a broken spirit drieth the bones." So remember the joy of the Lord is your strength! So don't allow anyone to steal your joy and break your spirit.

CHAPTER 5

THE FIGHT

As you read this chapter I believe you will find some answers that you've been looking for concerning yourself. I also believe you will move closer to your complete deliverance, so keep an open mind. We talked about the fact that evil DNA was introduced into the genes of man by fallen evil angels, to corrupt the purity of man's origin. The chapter fight is my understanding of what Apostle Paul was telling us about our natural makeup. Evil is present and God didn't put it there. Evil is Satan's plot to destroy the relationship between God and man. That's why it's so important to be blood washed and born again. Notice how the Apostle Paul explains this fight. The bible states in Romans 7:15-25, "For that which I do I allow not: for what I would, that do I not; but what I hate, that do I. If then I do that which I would not, I consent unto the law that it is good. Now then it is no more I that do it, but sin that dwelleth in me. For I know that in me (that is, in my flesh,) dwelleth no good thing: for to will is present with me; but how to perform that which is good I find not. For the good that I would I do not: but the evil which I would not, that I do. Now if I do that I would not, it is no more I that do it, but sin that dwelleth in me. I find then a law, that, when I would do good, evil is present with me. For I delight in the law of God after the inward man: but I see another law in my members, warring against the law of my mind, and bringing me into captivity to the law of sin which is my members. O wretched man that I am! Who shall deliver me from the body of this death? I thank God through Jesus Christ our Lord. So then with the mind I myself serve the law of God; but with the flesh the law of sin." What you have here is the fight, carnal and spiritual. None of us can escape this fight. The spirit has left its stamp on your soul which has imprinted your character, causing you to fight the DNA and generational curses which are ever present within you. Demonic spirits know this; because they've been watching you from birth and they're always impressing and trying to influence you. God has also assigned an angel to you, some call them guardian angels. We've spoken a lot about evil demonic spirits influencing and impressing on you. Guardian angels are doing the same by working in the rules of God, yet not interfering with your will. Apostle Paul spoke about the inward man. Let's look at this again; man is made up of body, soul and spirit. The body is the outer part of man, the spirit is the inner or inward man and the soul is caught between the two. Ezekiel 18:4 says, "Behold all souls are mine; as the soul of the father, so also the soul of the son is mine: the soul that sinneth, it shall die." So the precious commodity is the soul and all souls belong to God. Satan doesn't have any souls unless he steals them. Souls are transparent and I believe they're like a blank slate. The spirit is attached to the soul which is locked in the body, it takes these three body, soul and spirit, this is man's trinity. In my opinion this is a functioning man or living man. The bible states that man was created in the image of God, and Gods trinity is Father, Son and the Holy Ghost and these three make one, yet separate. This is amazing. The trinity functions as the power of one. The body sees things which become desirable to the flesh and by the soul being blank, the spirit impresses on it, which starts the outer man to react and as the outer man grows, (I'm talking about the flesh) it craves things of its own, such as food, water, baths, love, lust and passion all this has and imprint on the soul. The soul now becomes the puppet to the spirit as well as the body and depending on how the soul is developed, it becomes dark or good. You must understand that spirits are always present and being inside the body there are always desires because evil spirits are always trying to influencing your spirit. Let's use this scenario. Your friends have a party, one of your friends has a strong spirit, their personality is contagious, they're popular and they like you as a friend. You feel privileged to be in their company but they like to do drugs and because of social pressure, you try the drug. Now you're craving drugs and have no control, all because of an influencing spirit which was a demonic spirit using your friend to get to you. Now your body can't shake the habit and if you overdose and die in this sin, your soul will be lost in hell and you won't be able to cry your way out. You tried to do good but evil was present and many souls have been lost this way. (Even hanging around people who smoke could cause you to become tempted) These are tricks of the enemy that he uses to steal souls, causing cancer, drug addiction, STD's and alcoholism, just to name a few. Satan's kingdom is set up to steal your soul from God because he can't create or make a soul and he knows that God cherishes his souls. Now the Fight! 2 Corinthians 11:24-27 says, "Of the Jews five times received I forty stripes save one. Thrice was I beaten with rods, once was I stoned, thrice I suffered ship wreck, a night and a day I have been in the deep; In journeying often, in perils of waters, in perils of robbers, in perils by my own countrymen, in perils by the heathen, in perils in the city, in perils in the wilderness, in perils in the sea, in perils among false brethren; In weariness and painfulness, in watchings often, in hunger and thirst, in fasting often, in cold and nakedness." The bible says to fight the good fight of faith. Paul said in 2 Timothy 4:7-8, "I have fought a good fight, I have finished my course, I have kept the faith: Henceforth there is laid up for me a crown of righteousness, which the Lord, the righteous judge, shall give me at that day: and not to me only, but unto all them also that love his appearing." How much fight is in you? Because if you don't understand the game you'll lose the battle before you even get started. The world according to my understanding of the bible is set up by Satan. Everything is designed to entangle and draw you away from God, through fame, fortune, sex, drugs and politics of power. Satan doesn't want you to see clear and most don't. When your eyes become open and you see things for what they really are, you'll only want to get closer to God and this is when your fight really begins. Remember you were born in sin and shaped in iniquity, so your flesh desires the things of the world. You must always remember evil spirits are around you and the struggle is real. This isn't easy, if it was everybody would be saved. That's why you need the power and presence of God in your life. You must realize that Satan knows he's doomed and misery loves company, this is why Satan surrounds himself with stolen souls, because he feels like it hurts God. Notice what the bible says in Job 1:6-7, "Now there was a day when the sons of God came to present themselves before the Lord, and Satan came also among them. And the Lord said unto Satan, Whence comest thou? Then Satan answered the Lord, and said, From going to and fro in the earth, and from walking up and down in it." This is the conversation that took place in heaven between God and Satan. God realized and knew that Satan was trying to steal souls because God had just gone through that with Satan and one-third of the angels that Satan persuaded in heaven. I believe God allowed all that to go on in heaven to see who Satan could persuade because God didn't need them anyway. Once God saw who was persuaded by Satan, Michael and his host cast them out and now the same thing has taken place on earth with man. Have you ever wondered if God has had a conversation with Satan concerning you? Let's look at Job. God asked Satan. Have you considered my servant Job? Notice, God said servant. For God knew Job was sold out and couldn't be persuaded. Cold the same be said of you? Are you sold out? Are you weak to the cares of this wicked world? So Satan said to God in so many words, you cheaten, you got a hedge around Job, his house and everything he has. You blessed him with money, health, and a family. If Job didn't have your blessings, I'd make him curse you to your face. So God allowed Satan to have his way with Job and Job still held on to Gods unchanging hand and didn't get thrown in hell like Satan and the fallen angels. You do realize Satan hates you. Just like that mother that hates the sight of her child all because they look and act like their father. That's the same way Satan feels because you remind Satan of God every time he looks at you. Satan has no love for you but he will lie and say that he does. So how do you fight? The bible tells us in 2 Corinthians 10:4, "(The weapons of our warfare are not carnal, but mighty through God to the pulling down of strong-holds ;)" The battle is truly in the spirit. If you try to fight it in the flesh you will without question lose. Everything comes from the invisible. (The spiritual realm) God spoke the world into existence, just as God allowed Job or anyone else to be blessed. Job was in a spiritual war and Satan was trying to break Job's spirit and if Satan would've succeeded, Job would've lost his soul but Job understood all he had was his soul and all Job wanted to know was if a man die, shall he live again? Wealth will come and go, you can have more children, get more stuff, even a new wife or husband but you only have one soul. The bible tells us to put on the whole armor of God. Ephesians 6:11, 12 says, "Put on the whole armor of God, that ye may be able to stand against the wiles of the devil. For we wrestle not against flesh and blood, but against principalities, against powers, against the rulers of the darkness of this world, against spiritual wickedness in high places." Did you know there're demons assigned to you? (Principalities and spiritual wickedness) So you must first stand with truth. What is truth? ST. John 17:17 says, "Sanctify them through thy truth: thy word is truth." So we fight with the word of God. Proverbs says life and death is in the power of the tongue. So you must watch what you say; speak in faith knowing that God is with you. You must fight but in order to defeat an enemy you must know something about them. This is where your bible comes in. The bible is a book of faith, knowledge, wisdom and war. Exodus 15:3 says, "The Lord is a man of war: the Lord is his name." Even King David said God teaches his hands to war. So if you don't know your enemy, how can you defeat him? Even professional boxers have to study tapes of their opponents so that they'll know what to expect in the fight. I saw two men fighting in a movie, one was short and skinny, the other one was big with muscles. The short man kicked the big muscular man in the knee cap and then hit him in the throat; the fight was over, all because the short man knew what to do. The word of God is your sword, your faith is your shield and your breast plate is the righteousness and integrity you possess. If you stand on the word of God you'll have the peace of the gospel, knowing that you have made every preparation possible to win your battle. God will do the rest, I promise you this. God will not let you down; Satan knows this. That's why Satan has many different tactics and will switch up on you all the time. This is why you must remain prayerful because one of Satan tricks is the use of a false prophet. If you can't stop someone you simply confuse them by misleading them and sending them in the wrong direction, by mixing truth with lies. The church was silent as the minister testified of how he'd been around many so called men of God. He went on to say that he was invited to go golfing with some pastors who all had large congregations; he just knew he was in the in crowd. As he took a deep breath and said when they got on the golf course, the curse words that were coming out of their mouths put him in literal shock. He didn't know what to do but he knew this crowd was not for him. On that day he came to the realization that some men in his profession aren't spirit filled; the Holy Ghost is nowhere around them. This is why some whore chase, and find ways to make money off the church. Their personalities are so big, they've learned how to excite people and tell them exactly what they want to hear and instead of them preaching sin and salvation, they preach messages like when the clouds begin to cry or touched by your tears, all while allowing twerking, foot work and stepping in the house of God. These aren't the actions of a man called by God. This is a false prophet because there's no conviction and no deliverance. This is why the word of God says; wherefore by their fruit ye shall know them. Matthew 7:18 says, "A good tree cannot bring forth evil fruit, neither can a corrupt tree bring forth good fruit." So you must become fruit inspectors. When I buy my fruit, I look at it real good and you must do the same. You check them according to what the bible says. You know wrong when you see and hear it, so don't be afraid to ask questions because your soul is at stake. Are you a man of God who's guilty of preaching a certain way at church but allow your children and family do everything and anything? That's no good either. As a man of God you must practice what you preach and your house should be in order. You see the devil loves to hang out in the church when there's no fasting and praying. You must rebuke those demons and cast them out; they have no business in the true house of God. They're some churches the enemy is dug in so deep, you simply must leave. In this case, God will lead you. The more you know God the more you know and love a pure spirit. The bible says in Job 32:8-9, "But there is a spirit in man: and the inspiration of the Almighty giveth them understanding. Great men are not always wise: neither do the aged understand judgment." Real men of God are always seeking to understand more about God. When you're filled with the spirit of God, you will feel the power surge through your body; this is one of the greatest feelings you can have. As the Holy Ghost attaches to your common spirit and you become inspired and lead by the presence of God. Notice what the Bible says in Ephesians 1:17-23, "That the God of our Lord Jesus Christ, the Father of glory, may give unto you the spirit of wisdom and revelation in the knowledge of him: The eyes of your understanding being enlightened; that ye may know what is the hope of his calling, and what the riches of the glory of his inheritance in the saints, and what is the exceeding greatness of his power to us-ward who believe, according to the working of his mighty power, which he wrought in Christ, when he raised him from the dead, and set him at his own right in heavenly places, Far above all principality, and powers, and might, and dominion, and every name that is named, not only in this world, but also in that which is to come: and has put all things under his feet, and gave him to be the head over all things to the church, Which is his body the fullness of him that filleth all in all." Wow! That's the word of God. There shouldn't be any weak men of God because God is power and our job is the perfecting of the saints of God. Who you're taught by makes the difference. That's why you seek God for good leadership and a place that you can grow. So many saints have become bound by men of

God, who've allowed power to go to their head. I heard someone say, "If the devil can't cut you short he'll push you by." The enemy has pushed some men of God to the point where they want to control you because they themselves have a spirit of control and have become a tyrant, by telling you if you leave you aren't going to be blessed. That's speaking a curse on someone and some will go as far as to say I have your key. The bible says in 1 Corinthians 3:5-7, "Who then is Paul, and who is Apollos, but ministers by whom ye believed, even as the Lord gave to every man? I have planted, Apollos watered; but God gave the increase. So then neither is he that planteth any thing, neither he that watereth, but God that giveth the increase." Did you know you could outgrow a ministry? Yes. You can outgrow a ministry just as a plant can outgrow a pot and needs to be repotted into a larger pot, so it can further grow. You got saved under someone who only has a high school education and you have two masters, seeking a doctorate and you've been faithful for years. Now that God wants to elevate you, they've began to preach against education instead of praying a blessing over you and now you're hurt. Listen to me. This happens more than you think. It is old school thinking, which we call stinking thinking and God isn't in it. Be sweet and not bitter because the hand of God is moving you up and just pray for them, for they've hit their peak. Tell it! One of the members shouted out as the Evangelist testified of how he was blackballed because of his ability to preach a more in-depth message with revelation. He testified of how the members began to gravitate towards the message and how he was told he was too deep and to just preach faith. He went on to say how the spirit of jealousy was exposed and at that point he realized he had outgrown the pot. As a result other pastors that his pastor had influence over would no longer support him, all except one. (God always has one) The hurt was horrific! This experience he said he'd wish upon no one. As he went on to say, you must trust the God in your life and not allow yourself to become bound because they will try to hinder you and make you an example so that others will fear and that's not God. That's the spirit of man using the spirit of control and now the devil gets in causing depression, hurt, bitterness and slander. Paul had forty men against him, they vowed a curse and they wouldn't eat or drink until he was killed. That's a lot of negative energy in those spirits. People will pray against you but if you're in the will of God, it will not work. So stay in his will and obey God. You must know when you need help; in this case you should seek someone who knows how to pray in the spirit. This is a spiritual warfare and prayer is very important because it's a life line. (It's like building up steam or hot air in a hot air balloon; the more air, the higher the balloon) You must be able to pray in the spirit so you can reach beyond earth's realm, like Daniel prayed. Satan will try to hinder your prayer or delay your answer but you must be patient for your answer. The angel Gabriel was detained by the demonic forces of Satan for twenty-one days. Michael one of the chief angels had to come and help Gabriel and Daniel got his answer. In his wait, Daniel never lost hope in what he believed, he didn't allow his faith to die and Daniel trusted in the word God had revealed to him. The bible states in Psalm 119:49, 50, "Remember the word unto thy servant, upon which thou has caused me to hope. This is my comfort in my affliction:

for thy word hath quickened me." The definition of quickened is to be brought alive. The word along with the spirit of God creates life and change, so when God has spoken to you through his word, revelation, dream or prophetically. He continues to give life to that seed of hope through the preaching and teaching of his word. This is the connection of the quickening and the power that it brings forth springs your faith to life. The bible says in Romans 8:10-13, "And if Christ be in you, the body is dead because of sin; but the Spirit is life because of righteousness. But if the Spirit of him that raised up Jesus from the dead dwell in you, he that raised up Christ from the dead shall also quicken your mortal bodies by his Spirit that dwelleth in you. Therefore, brethren, we are debtors, not to the flesh, to live after the flesh. For if ye live after the flesh, ye shall die: but if ye through the spirit do mortify the deeds of the body, ye shall live." Mortify means to subdue the body or its needs and desires by self-denial and discipline. When you yield to the flesh your spirit is subdued and your spiritual man has no control. You're walking spiritually dead because the flesh is the master; this is what I call the Frankenstein Syndrome. This means you have become spiritually dead because you've aloud your faith to die and as a result you've become a walking corpse. You're dead to the spirit and controlled by the flesh. Flesh is powerful; you were born in it, so it had you first. The flesh craves and has very strong desires. That's why you can have a nice car and still want another one, you can have a closet full of clothes, (Some still with tags on them) yet your flesh desires more, you have a good woman but you desire another. In dealing with the flesh you will not win, this is why you must depend on the power of the Comforter, The Holy Ghost. It is essential to your spiritual survival; it's the power of God. The bible states in St. John 14:26, "But the Comforter, which is the Holy Ghost, whom the father will send in my name," Acts 1:8, "But ye shall receive power, after that the Holy Ghost is come upon you:" This is unlimited power a never ending charge. The flesh is self-charging; this is why you must feed the spirit because only the spirit of God can give you the charge necessary to come alive. You may not see it but there's a continual battle going on. Everybody is fighting their own battles and God and the host of heaven is helping. When it gets too hard, the Lord knows how much you can bare. So when the enemy comes in like a flood, lift up the standard of God, don't backslide or give up, tie a knot at the end of the rope and hold on because help is on the way. Don't stop praying. Remember little prayer little power, much prayer much power because prayer is the key and faith unlocks the door and behind the door is your blessing. So you must train for the fight because the fight is coming to you whether you want to fight or not, it's coming. You have something Satan wants and that something is your soul. The fight is fought in the spirit but it manifest in the flesh. Notice what the bible says in Job 22:3, "Is it any pleasure to the almighty, that thou are righteous? Or is it gain to him, that thou makest thou ways perfect?" God wants to see you make it, he didn't sacrifice his son for no reason and Jesus didn't send back the Holy Ghost for you to ignore him. This is the plan of salvation but the question is how much fight is in you? I saw two dogs fight in a movie, one dog was a pit-bull, the other was a rock weller. I said to myself that little dog can't beat that big dog, but he did. You see it was the fight that was in the dog, not the size of the dog. Listen to me, the fight must be in you and you must know how to fight but remember the weapons of our warfare are not carnal; this is the fight Daniel and Paul fought. God is concerned about you living right because God wants you to come home with him in heaven and not end up in hell. You must understand that they're rules and laws in everything and the bible is your guide line.

CHAPTER 6

WHO DO YOU LOVE MOST?

2 Timothy 3:2, "For men shall be lovers of their own selves, covetous, boasters, proud, blasphemers, disobedient to parents, unthankful, unholy," We're living in these times but you've heard this before. So let us focus on lovers of their own selves. They love themselves so much that they take their on pictures called selfies. This is the selfies generation; people have now fallen in love with themselves to the point that they tattoo their bodies, face, and neck. If that's not enough they pierce their nose, tongue, lips, navel and even their private parts. (Lord have mercy) How can you get in the spirit if you're so into the flesh? Satan has set up his kingdom where flesh is king. Even music has subliminal messages hidden within the beats; along with sexual lyrics, as they boast of how proud they are of their lifestyle. It seems like life is cheap to them but who do you love? Are you caught up in this or are you looking to be caught up in this lifestyle? Modern day gospel rap has now infiltrated the church. We now have gospel rap but there's a thin line between gospel rap and worldly rap. I'm not saying not to

enjoy the blessings of God just don't forget about God. If you put God first he will give you balance in your life and victory over the flesh. (Paul said there are no good things in my flesh) The flesh likes to look good and feel good but remember this one thing, the flesh will die. Its testimony time and the Evangelist stands and says, "He was a fashion model and caught up in himself, as he describes himself as standing six feet two inches, a slim hundred and seventy-five pounds, always traveling with a wardrobe, as he changed his clothes two to three times a day. He tells how he was bound by jazz and R&B; he was a lover of himself and anything that would make his flesh happy, from drugs to women. He goes on to say how his mother who's a real prayer warrior along with her friends, prayed him out of the hand of the enemy. As he begins to give God the glory while stating whenever he sees young men full of themselves like he was; he says a prayer for them because somebody prayed for him." Times have changed and the fashion world is so different. We now have high end designers who jeans cost as much as $500, gym shoes ranging from $200 and up, designer belts that cost over $200 and would you believe some pay $100 for a t-shirt and $75 for a base-ball cap. Wow! What a change in times from dress shoes, slacks and nick nick shirts, yet none the less lovers of self. It's time to find you some God and get delivered from self because time is winding up. You can live now and die forever or except Christ and live forever. Take your pick but my question to you still remains, Who Do You Love Most? You can get the victory over your flesh. Is it going to be easy? No. Anything worth having is never easy. So let's start now, right now. That generational curse must be broken. You're influenced by seducing spirits that work through flesh but you must bring your flesh into subjection through the power of God. We all must come this way and there're no short cuts. For you never know when someone will start shooting at a party or get jealous because you took their woman or man. You must understand that some people have evil demonic forces that operate through them and they will kill you and your soul will end up in hell forever in flames. I believe the economic system is set up by Satan who truly rules and controls this world. I also believe the educational system is set up were the best education is too expensive for the average family and only the privileged can get in. (There's always a percentage they allow in to keep from looking so bias) Yes. These people control everything because Satan controls them. This is real; nothing is by accident, it's all by design, down to the colors in a restaurant. Yes, something as simple as colors. Did you know that certain colors will arouse your appetite? Just as certain colors will run you out of a bathroom. Did you know if you put less mirrors in the women's bathroom they will spend less time? Colors have power of influence and colors also set moods. When the boss gives a speech if he wants to show power, he'll wear a red tie and if he wants trust, he'll wear a blue tie. Satan understands the human mind and he influences people through music, television and fashion. Satan wants you to show your flesh because it promotes the spirit of lust. The fashion industry tells you what's in style for the upcoming season and then floods the market with it and it becomes hard to find anything else. Everyone is at attention as the first lady testifies, "Of how being a woman of holiness it's hard to find a blouse that's not cut to low or a skirt without a split. She goes on to say that in today's fashion world it's almost impossible to find modest apparel but as women of God we most hold the standard of God and not allow the fashion world to cause us to lower our standards. As she takes a breath and says saved women don't show their bust, they don't wear blouses off their shoulders and they don't wear tight skirts that show their knees and panty lines. She went on to testify that when God gets ahold to you and you align yourself with the word of God you as a woman of God will not allow Satan to use you as an object of lust but instead you become an example of Godliness." Let's take a look at how the world promotes alcohol. The very same cognac that you got delivered from twenty, thirty, forty years ago Satan now uses the lure of honey bees and sweet green apples to attract the new generation. Think about it for a moment, it's the same cognac but a different hook. Did you know social pressure will cause you to lose yourself in the moment? The moment has now taken control because you've already been programed through the music, the movies, the television and the fashion world. So you've now become lost in the darkness and now these evil spirits exercise power over you. At this point you've become caught up in the maze of life, which has claimed countless souls. Yes, Satan's world is beautiful with lots of pleasure and fun, which causes you to feel free and released from your troubles but it's all an illusion. That freedom becomes bondage because you're driven by evil spirits that have set you up and have centuries of experience in doing so. These evil spirits know you better then you know yourself. Trust me when I tell you that you're not there by mistake, it was a well-designed plan and now the only thing that can help you is the true power of God.

Remember the enemy knows this and has his church out there with his false prophets to make you believe that the church is no better. Satan wants you to believe that the church is full of crooked preachers and all they want is your money. This is the mindset Satan wants you to have but God told Elisha in 1 Kings 19:18, "Yet I have left me seven thousand in Israel, all the knees which have not bowed unto Baal, and every mouth which hath not kissed him." So you think you're the only one that feels that way? God has his people out here but you must seek ye the Lord while he is near, call upon him while he may be found and don't stop praying because you will get delivered. ST. John 3:17, says "For God sent not his son into the world to condemn the world; but that the world through him might be saved." So the question is Who Do You Love Most? God or the world? I'm not trying to tell you it's easy but when you have a made up mind and you're determined to be free, God has an angel by your side that will help you. So when your flesh rares up, which it will. You must be able to bring it under subjection and obey the will of God. Nobody will twist your arm, you have free will to do whatever you want to do but I pray you make the right choice and say get thee behind me Satan and move forward in God. I hope you will accept the will of God and start running your race because we all must run, with the understanding that the race is not given to the swift, neither is it given to the strong but to them that endure to the end. (You're reading this for a reason) God is saying run and don't stop for if you love God you'll make the right choice. You must realize this isn't a game and these demons aren't playing with you. All these movies that come out about paranormal activities and true stories about people being possessed by evil spirits aren't a lie. You see and hear about these things and you push them off but for everyone they show you on the big screen, there're thousands that they didn't show you. They only show the ones they think they can make money off of, while warning you at the same time. Seducing spirits need a vessel to use just like the spirit of God uses a vessel. You're a vessel but which spirit will use you? Will it be the Holy Spirit or an evil spirit? For one will win and there's only heaven or hell. Read your bible it's more than just words on a page. God's spirit is released through the Holy Bible. When Matthew, Mark, Peter and John wrote their part of the bible they were inspired by the spirit of God. The world can't comprehend the fact that there's a spirit in God's word and that spirit carries the power of God. As you read and believe that spirit can be released and you'll realize that something super-natural other than words and thoughts are present. The Holy Spirit itself comes over you when you allow your spirit to be embraced and make a connection with the Holy Spirit. When this takes place you'll began to break and brokenness is where your understanding begins. The bible says in 2 Corinthians 3:6, "Who also hath made us able ministers of the new testament; not of letter, but of the spirit; for the letter killeth, but the spirit giveth life." For without Gods spirit on these words the bible would be just like any other book. These men of God were moved by the Holy Spirit which inspired the writings of the scriptures. The Holy Spirit is eternal and alive within these pages and waiting for you to discover your destiny in God. You must first open your heart and the spirit of God will incorporate his nature in you little by little, until you get a grip and start to grow. God's way is the way of the spirit touching our spirit. This contact allows you to have spiritual growth in God as you read his word and there's no limit on God. If you can believe it, you can receive it and as a result your fellowship with God begins to become so intimate and private, that your heart becomes sealed. Ephesians 1:13, says "In whom ye also trusted, after that ye heard the word of truth, the gospel of your salvation: in whom also after that ye believed, ye were sealed with the Holy Spirit of promise," (Amen, I tell you the promises of God are yea and Amen) You enter into a secret place where you're hid in Christ with God and the only way Satan can get to you is if you break the seal. (Now there's a hedge around you like it was with Job) You become untouchable because you're Gods property; a part of a royal priesthood. Satan can throw fiery darts but that's all he can do. He can't lay a hand on you without going through God. (Some call it the ark of safety) Remember Satan and his demons will always try to lure you out through friends and family but now that you have a different mind and a changed heart, they simply won't understand you because you're no longer a part of their world. The scales have been lifted off your eyes and you see things different. Literally somebody said "I looked at my hands and they looked new, I looked at my feet and they did too, I looked at the sky and it was bluer then blue and when I looked in the mirror, I said who are you?" You must know that there's up keep to maintain and the battle is in your will because there will be temptation. Satan gave birth to the second will but remember God created order and one accord; it's so unfortunate that now there're billions of wills that differ from Gods will among mankind and it all began with Satan and his will against

God. Satan simply wanted to do things his way and the way he desired. So Satan has made it his business to always confuse the will of God, so man can stay lost in his desires but God said lo, I come in the volume of a book. (This is to help you know the true will of God) If God spared not the angels, what do you think he'll do to you? God is just and has made a way for us all to escape, by sending his only begotten Son the Living Word. So don't allow your will or desires to cause you to end up in the lake of fire with Satan. This is real my reader, I love you and have taken this time by the leading of the Holy Spirit to be another voice crying out against that terrible day. You must realize that demons are real, Satan is real and there's another realm in the spirit. You're just a small piece in the puzzle of life, yet the picture isn't complete without you. So let your light shine so others may see and do your part in helping someone else understand how severe this is. Eternity can't be counted, it's always one more day then you can ever think of. So the question still remains, Who Do You Love Most? You must fight and hold on to what God has given you because you have the weapon to defeat Satan, which is the blood of Jesus. For there's power in the blood Jesus shed; the incorruptible blood covers us; in the spirit you're covered, so plead the blood of Jesus. The word plead means; to make action or legal proceeding or stated fact alleging the fact. What fact? The fact that Jesus has given us power through our confession and faith, along with the authority to use the blood to back up Satan. This further lets me know the importance of being covered with the blood of Christ because all of us have a part of this evil inside us and some more than others (So you can never measure the evil in a person) because Satan and his fallen angels infected us. The fact remains that it's not about religion or your denomination but being washed in the blood of the lamb, which became the final sacrifice for man to be reconciled back to his God because none of Satan's spawn will get through the gates of heaven. Only the blood washed; those that are cleansed in his blood, the pure untainted power. So there's no excuse because the work has already been done, the sacrifice has already been made, the instructions have been written and the example made. So it's now off God and on you because you have the victory through the blood of Jesus. Now you can fully understand the importance of the virgin birth of the Son of God and him shedding his blood. This was the only way to redeem man; Gods master piece. So plead the blood of Jesus against Satan at all times, plead the blood of Jesus over your mind, over your heart, over your children, over your finances, over your health and over your marriage. Plead the blood, the blood, the blood because the word reminds you that greater is in you and you are the sheep that possess the shepherd and there's always a way to escape. The bible says in James 4:7, "Resist the devil, and he will flee from you."

CHAPTER 7

GOD IS NOT A TRICKSTER

When some preachers preach they have the tendency to come off as if God has tricks. God is Not a Trickster and God doesn't need to trick anybody, especially those who love him. This is why you must be careful who you sit under in ministry. The fact of the matter is life has to have balance. God is the architect of life; he deals in life matters throughout the universe, where they're ups, downs, good, bad, hot, cold, love and hate. The fact of the matter is, life has to have balance and the truth of the matter is, everything that's black and white has to meet somewhere in the middle. While the leveling is being done this is your grey area. Each one has a middle where they collide balancing them both and this is the area of turbulence. God said in Romans 9:18, "Therefore hath he mercy on whom he will have mercy, and whom he will he hardeneth." Paul also said in the same chapter verse fourteen, "What shall we say then? Is there unrighteousness with God? God forbid." Verse fifteen says, "For he sayeth to Moses, I will have mercy on whom I will have mercy, and I will have compassion on whom I will have compassion." God makes the hard decisions because life demands it. Pharaoh came out the vessel of dishonor and Moses the vessel of honor. Moses being the vessel of honor suffered on the back side of the dessert in his making, while Pharaoh continued in his life of luxury. Being in the center is also hard, no one wants to be tossed to the black, most of us want to be tossed to the white but the spiral of life sometimes works based on our choices. God has a perfect will for you but by you having a will of your on you sometimes choose to follow your on desires, which has an adverse effect. You knew in the beginning that woman or man was bad news but you choose to get involved with them anyway and now you want God to clean up the mess behind you, only for you to make a bad decision in something else. (Instead of you praying Lord let your will be done in my life lead me and guide me) This takes unraveling. Think about it, if Jesus would've yielded in the Garden of Gethsemane his flesh would've had him bound for eternity. Jesus had to fight the full weight of the flesh because he was locked in the body his father prepared for him and Jesus asked his father, is there any other way? Jesus came through the fight of the flesh and said never the less let thy will be done. Just as Jesus felt the full weight of the flesh and fought it, you must also fight your flesh. The bible says in Hebrews 4:15, "For we have not an high priest which cannot be touched with the feelings of our infirmities; but was in all points tempted like as we are, yet without sin." We as believers don't practice sin and if you happen to sin, Jesus hung bleed and died for that reason. This is why you need the Comforter. For sometimes the only way out is the hard way but you must stay the course that you know is right in your heart and endure hardness as a good soldier. Being a soldier sometimes requires great patience and waiting can be taxing on your mind, spirit and body. The fatigue can seem unbearable. This is what happened to Daniel when Satan held up the answer to his prayer for 21 days but he endured hardness as good soldier and God sent help. Notice what the bible says in Daniel 10:12, 13 "Then said he unto me, Fear not, Daniel for from the first day that thou didst set thine heart to understand, and to chasten thyself before thy God, thy words were heard, and I am come for thy words, But the prince of the kingdom of Persia withstood me one and twenty days: but, lo, Michael, one of the chief princes, came to help me; and I remained there with the king of Persia." This must have been really difficult to Daniel because he knew God heard his prayer. I imagine Daniel couldn't make sense out of not getting an answer from God. Satan had casted a dark shadow over Daniel by hindering the answer to his prayer. Sometimes its not you but it's the battle on the other side. So if you're doing your part rest assure God will do his but you must wait because there're things going on in the spirit that you can't see or hear. So don't doubt God because God is Not a Trickster. God is fixing it for you but you must allow the time necessary for God to get the job done in your life. What if Daniel would've got frustrated, begin to doubt and gave up like most of us do? (O ye of little faith) You must learn to wait under the dark cloud that Satan has casted over you until God clears it up. Notice what the bible states in Micah 7:7, 8 "Therefore I will look unto the Lord; I will wait for the God of my salvation: my God will hear me. Rejoice not in me, O mine enemy: when I fall, I shall arise; when I sit in darkness, the Lord shall be a light unto me." When Satan cast darkness over you remember Micah and know the Lord shall be a light unto you. If Satan tries to afflict you with sickness, hinder your finances, attack your children or destroy your marriage these things become shadows of darkness. There're many shades and levels of darkness, just as there's many colors. There's a white and a winter white there're both white but one is darker than the other. (I'm trying to get you to understand that a trial is a trial no matter what the level is) When you're going through something you're in a dark place and sometimes God will put or allow you to be in a dark place, just as God did with Job. Job was in the darkest place man can be in and job only wanted to know one thing. The bible says in Job 14:14, "If a man die, shall he live again? All the days of my appointed time will I wait, till my change come." Once again we come to the word wait. You see God has a reason for everything he does and through the story of Job you learn that God used Job for bragging rights and Job set under that darkness until he was delivered. Daniel's darkness wasn't as dark as Job's darkness but they both had to wait until God cleared that dark cloud. So don't faint in the mist of your waiting because too much is given, much is required. Notice what the bible says in Isaiah 40:28-31, "Hast thou not known? Hast thou not heard, that the everlasting God, the Lord, the Creator of the ends of the earth, fainteth not, neither is weary? there is no searching of his understanding. He giveth power to the faint; and to them that have no might he increaseth strength. Even the youths shall faint and be weary, and the young men shall utterly fall: But they that wait upon the Lord shall renew their strength; they shall mount up with wings as eagles; they shall run, and not be weary; and they shall walk, and not faint." God is Not a Trickster. The problem is you just give in to easy. This is a war; you never know when a war will be over but you know one thing for sure there will be casualties. Even the youth shall fall because for some of them the world is simply too powerful and they have no patience, as they become consumed with the social pressures of life. Paul said in Philippians 4:11, "Not that I speak in respect of want: for I have learned, in whatsoever state I am, therewith to be content." The bible states in 1 Timothy 6:6, "But godliness with contentment is great gain." Notice how Paul said I have learned this. Paul is letting you know through the scripture that it doesn't come over night. You learn as you go and grow but the problem is some of you stop growing because you become impatient and the dark cloud consumes you and as a result you choose to go another way, instead of the way God chose because you allowed your faith to waiver and you became wounded by the trail. So while you're under your dark clouds of life don't spiritually bleed out, ask for prayer and seek counsel so you can hold on because help is on the way. Life is just life, so you must find enjoyment where you can because the dark black side doesn't care their going to do it to death and then for them it's over. You see they get theirs now and pay later but you live the life to live again and though you think life isn't fair sometimes, I can assure you it has to balance itself. It's unfortunate that some pay more than others but the turbulence of the grey must exist and there's nothing easy about being in the middle of anything, especially life. So make wise choices because life doesn't mind making them for you and it will, because it's a machine set in place designed by God that never stops running, in which you can only pray works in your favor. Hezekiah got God to change the flow of the spiral and tossed him fifteen more years of life but Hezekiah had something to present before God, a life. When you put God first he can change the spiral of life because he controls the machine. We're living in a hard time in the world as we know it, so you must learn to reinvent yourself more than once or twice. There was a time when you could start a job or career and retire. Not anymore, if you get ten years it's a miracle. So if you don't learn how to shift into survival mode you won't make it and pride must go out the window. Life has a way of coming full circle if you stay true to yourself and always be the best of who you are, while surviving the waves of life because sometimes the waves come high and heavy but the real you will come through. People are losing their faith in God and trusting in only what they see and feel. The atmosphere is full of negativity and unbelief and you can feel it but despite the dark clouds you must cherish the presence of God and allow God to work through you. You must contend for the faith which was delivered to the saints because your faith is all you have. Hebrews 11:6, says "But without faith it is impossible to please him;" Notice what the scripture says in Hebrews 11:1, "Now faith is the substance of things hoped for, the evidence of things not seen." Not seen means invisible; which means impossible to see, not visible, incapable by nature to be seen with the naked eye but that doesn't mean it's not there or exists. Please note what the bible says in the third verse "Through faith we understand that the worlds were framed by the word of God, so that things which are seen were not made of things which do appear." The connection is faith and you get faith by hearing which allows you to believe in God's word, which stimulates God interest in what you're believing him for. Your faith becomes a wave. Let's use an ether wave for example, ether meaning upper air, pure air, a space filling substance. (You can't see air but you can feel it) The wind is a powerful and invisible force, the faster it moves, the more powerful it becomes but God is greater than the wind. An ether wave is an electromagnetic wave that exists in the air moving throughout the universe. When you pick up your phone and dial a number the ether wave connects you to whomever you're calling, whether they're in Africa, California or Las Vegas. You have the confidence that an unseen wave will connect you to the person in whom you're dialing and now with face-time you can talk to the person and see them at the same time in this case the invisible produce the visible. God is greater than an ether wave and as you build your faith it becomes your substance. (Your ether wave) When you confess the word of God you give life which creates the substance of faith mixed along with the word of God, in which you get the attention of the ancient one. The only way to move God is through the spoken word because there's power in his word. God spoke the world into existence. God said let there be light and immediately light shined in the mist of darkness. So speak your way out of your dark place and build your power by building your knowledge of God's word and free yourself from the bondage of unbelief. You must know that God is greater, for greater is he that is in you then he that is in the world. The world has the ether wave and we have our faith. So build yourself on the most holy faith and get away from unbelieving people. Stay away from negativity and generate your force of faith that you may receive the promises of God. You can break through all this negativity in the world but you must believe in God our Father and our Lord Jesus Christ and know that he is a rewarder of those whom diligently seek him.

CHAPTER 8

GODS PEOPLE DON'T PRACTICE SIN

There comes a time when you must take responsibility for your actions and your desires but the truth of the matter is some of you are simply not ready; you want your cake and eat it to. (Here's an example of what I mean) A person graduates from seminary school with all their degrees including a doctorate in theology. This same person also has their own law firm and wants to be big in ministry and because they spent all that time in seminary school they feel as though they deserve it. As a result they become bitter toward other successful pastors who they deem less educated than them. I applaud those with seminary schooling and doctorates; maybe I'll get an honorary one day but this is a matter of the heart and God knows the intense of a man's heart. (You can fool everybody else but you will never be able to fool God) I'm using this example to say education is good but you must give God a life because Gods People

Don't Practice Sin! (I'm not done with this example so stay behind me) You can't be a person who's a whore-monger and a liar and hold God accountable for your short comings in ministry. Men of God, women of God and the people of God don't practice sin; children stumble and fall but it's never their intention to scare their knee. When this happens they go to their father or mother crying and mama or daddy put a bandage over it after they clean it up and the child goes on not looking to fall again. This is what Christ did when he died on the cross for us and we accepted him as our Lord and Savior. Christ cleans you up through his blood and gives you a change of heart. Christ knew it wouldn't be easy because he knows the flesh is weak so he sent back the Holy Ghost to give you power not to yield to sin. That's why you must have a made up mind and be ready for the fight with the understanding that you're not a slave to sin but the truth is some of you are simply not ready and you want to blame God. It's not God's fault that you have desires for the world and a loose life because those that are truly saved and spirit filled don't practice sin. As babes in Christ you may scare your spiritual knees but as you grow you mature and the more God you get the stronger you become. This is why as a child of God you must watch where you plant your seeds and where you worship. You don't want to become a personality worshipper and get caught up in how someone looks, how they dress, how they walk, talk and their mannerisms, which will lure you into their lifestyle and draw you away from God. So you must therefore give God a life, Holy and acceptable which is your reasonable service to God. This is why you look for good ground to plant into. (When I say plant I'm speaking in terms of your offerings and tithes) If you draw from good ground you should plant more seeds in that same fertile ground. I don't understand those who want to buy chicken from the chicken house and go eat it at the hamburger house. This is dear to my heart because it seems like a growing trend. I've witnessed a woman of God pray for many people and God answered the prayers sometimes immediately. On one occasion a young lady came to this woman of God and asked her to pray for her daughter who had an illness. The young lady stated to the woman of God, my pastor's wife doesn't believe like you do. The woman of God prayed and believed God with the young lady and the child got healed of that illness. (To God be all the glory) Do you think the young lady planted a seed in that good ground? The answer is no. Instead she took her money and support right back to the ministry that didn't believe. (This is only one of many experiences I witnessed) As you grow older you should reach a place in God where the very life that people see and have heard about pertaining to you, should demand their respect. As you become a walking memorial for Christ sin should be far from you and if you've been blessed to see seventy, eighty or ninety years of age you should have victory over lust, cussing, fussing, backbiting and gossiping. You should be seeking God to help someone find their way or are you trying to live again through someone else's life because you're bitter at how your life turned out? (Loose here!) The devil shouldn't be able to use someone at that age but we find more and more that people at that age are still confused to what they believe and that's unfortunate. They're still looking and fighting for an opportunity for themselves, instead of providing opportunities for someone else. (Lord we need an old school revival) Satan has managed to confuse America and the world; you can go to a church that has two-hundred members and find ten different bible interpretations of the same scripture. It's time to pray, be bold and focus on the kingdom of God as people of God because we do become our brother's keeper, if he seeks our help in his search for the truth. What is truth? God's word is truth. The bottom line is as a child of God you shouldn't practice sin because Gods People Don't Practice Sin. Rejecting the will of God is serious because your soul is at stake, so it's time to clean up your spiritual mess and let God do the rest, so he can make you one of his best because there's one thing for sure and that is, Hell is real! If the rich man could come back he would tell you don't come to this place because hell is a place of torture and torment. Hell is a place where worms don't die and the smoke from the sulfur is so thick, you continuously gasp for air never being able to catch a full breath. Hell has levels and chambers with real demons not make believe demons. Demon that stands eight feet tall half beast with only one thing in mind your torment, as it pulls out your guts while you scream through eternity and that's not all it feeds you excrement, while you lay in putrid vomit, full of worms and that demon is assigned to you for eternity in your cell of hell and that's just one level. All because you choice the pleasure of sin but when sin is finished, it brings forth death. Notice what the bible says in Isaiah 62: 9-12, "But they that have gathered it shall eat it, and praise the Lord; and they that have brought it together shall drink it in the courts of my holiness. Go through, go through the gates; prepare ye the way of the people; cast up, cast up the highway; gather out the stones; lift up a standard for the people. Behold, the Lord hath proclaimed unto the end of the world, Say ye to the daughter of Zion, Behold, thy salvation cometh; behold, his reward is with him, and his work before him. And they shall call them, The holy people, The redeemed of the Lord; and thou shalt be called, Sought out, a city not forsaken." In this passage God is talking about his people and his people are called Holy. The problem is people don't like being called holy or associated with holiness. A Holiness Church feels odd to someone with a free spirit; a person who has loose standards and no moral values. As you hear the testimonies of how God has worked miracles in people lives it can make you believe in a miracle for yourself. So when you go for prayer little do you know the seed of righteousness is planted in your soul and you become like a fish with a hook in his jaw. The fish can swim and fight as long as he wants but when he gets a little tired the fisherman reels him in a little closer. This is how God does you through life experiences, as you get tired of the fight or struggle God pulls you a little closer, whether it's through your first heartbreak, near miss accident or affliction. St. John 6:44 says, "No man can come to me, except the Father which hath sent me draw him: and I will raise him up at the last day." You can't just turn God on and off like a faucet. If you're fortunate enough God will draw you to him to become one of his children. Jesus also said in St. John 6: 37, 38, "All that the Father giveth me shall come to me; and him that cometh to me I will in no wise cast out. For I came down from heaven, not to do mine own will, but the will of him that sent me." This is why Gods people are also called his chosen. To be chosen by God is the greatest thing that could ever happen to someone because God looks at the heart and your inner man. So get out your mind that you can get God when you want him because it doesn't work that way, you must be drawn unto God. So when you stand in the halls of heaven in the courts of Holiness, you won't be there by accident because you can't slick your way into heaven. Heaven is a prepared place for a prepared people. (You're either in or you're not) There will be no mistakes, Christ knows them the father has assigned to him and they will not be the one's practicing sin because Gods people don't say anything, go anywhere or let their good be evil spoken of. We are humans living in this wicked world surrounded by sin just as Jesus was, so each day is a faith walk as we trust God to show us a way to escape the vortex of life on this side of heaven. This is as real as it gets because the world plays for keeps and it's governed by the opposing force; the king of sin, the father of lies who has one thing in mind, your soul. Satan makes it very hard to resist his set up but God understands the limits of the flesh and will not allow you to steal his righteousness. So when your flaws show up God shows out with his grace, mercy and long suffering because it's not of your righteousness but the righteousness of God working through you with the power of the Holy Ghost. So open your heart and learn of him, receive his spirit and rely on the power of the Holy Ghost to give you power to resist a sinful lifestyle and guide you into the halls of heaven to receive a place on Holy Ghost Blvd or Sanctified Ave.

BECAUSE I HAVE HOPE

Psalms 119:74, "They that fear thee will be glad when they see me; because I have hope in thy word." Here David is speaking to believers that fear God. (Those that stay within the boundaries of the word) There are some who will step outside the boundaries because they have no fear, as they play russian-roulette with heaven and hell, tempting God like a mouse playing with a trap that has a big piece of cheese on it. The mouse doesn't have the patience to wait until somebody drops a crumb on the floor, just like some of you who can't wait on God to provide. (So you jump out there and pop!) Those that fear God are glad to see someone strong in the Lord that has come through and received a breakthrough and continues to walk in hope of receiving more, so when you see them you're glad. When you walk in a place does somebody feel glad to see you? Do you bring hope with your presence because of the life you live before your brothers and sisters in Christ? You must hold to the faith that was delivered to you. Your faith shouldn't be like trying to hold on to a slippery fish; you should have a firm grip. For some have grown weary and have lost hope in the miracles God have promised them. Paul said in Romans 8:24, 25 "For we are saved by hope: but hope that is seen is not hope: for what a man seeth, why doeth he yet hope for it? But if we hope for that we see not, then do we with patience wait for it. So in our patience we gain experience; and experience hope:" You must allow patience to have its perfect work in your life. David said "I waited patiently on the Lord and he inclined unto me." So wait on God and move when God moves. At this point in your spiritual life you enter into the place where Abraham was. Romans 4:18 says, "Who against hope believed in hope, that he might become the father of many nations, according to that which was spoken, so shall thy seed be." Abraham at age eighty-six and Sarah couldn't see conceiving a child with Sarah being past the flower of age. God is just that promised and can recreate the womb to blossom again in a new season. (Glory to God) You have a new season coming and your season is now because the hope of glory is upon you. So embrace this new place in faith and walk in the newness of your new season. It's now your time and greater is he that is in you. So let your light so shine that men and women may see the hope you walk in.

WHEN YOU SEE GODS DELIGHT

2nd Chronicles 9:1, "And when the queen of Sheba heard of the fame of Solomon, she came to prove Solomon with hard questions at Jerusalem." Notice in verse one queen Sheba came as a skeptic. As you read further in the chapter you'll find that queen Sheba mind was changed as she got to know the man of God and saw Gods delight in him. Verse 8, 9 says "Blessed be Lord thy God, which delighted in thee to set thee on his throne, to be king for the Lord thy God: because thy God loved Israel, to establish them forever, therefore made he thee king over them, to do judgment and justice. And she gave the king one hundred and twenty talents of gold, and of spices great abundance, and precious stones: neither was there any such spice as the queen of Sheba gave King Solomon." Queen Sheba saw that it was God who set Solomon over his people. God sets a man in position and it's God who predestines each of our lives, so live in what God has provided for you. Queen Sheba saw one greater and there was no jealousy, only respect. Not only did queen Sheba respect Solomon's position she planted a seed in it, by adding to what he already had. She understood God was with Solomon and it was good ground to plant in, so she invested in the good ground expecting a harvest. We shouldn't be envious of what someone else has but instead we should examine how they got it. We should be as fruit inspectors and check out the fruits of their life. The bible says, "You shall know them by the fruit they bear" If it's God you'll know and you'll see because of their life and their speech. They'll be lifting up the spirit of the Lord, insightful, full of wisdom and giving God the glory. If it's not God you'll know because their speech will betray them with vile and ungodly words because sweet and bitter water can't come out the same faucet. Queen Sheba was checking out the people around Solomon and saw that they were happy, they had healthy spirits, they weren't depressed and they didn't feel trapped against their will. May be we should take a lesson from the world. When they see a successful movie star they say no charge because their presence is enough. So when a real man of God comes in your presence plant a seed no matter how small because that's good ground. Take a lesson from the Queen and be blesse

SLOW OF HEART TO BELIEVE

St. Luke 24:25-27 "Then he said unto them, O fools, and slow of heart to believe all that the prophets have spoken: Ought not Christ to have suffered these things, and to enter into his glory? And beginning at Moses and all the prophets, he expounded unto them in all the Scriptures the things concerning himself." Slow meaning: lacking readiness, promptness or willingness, registering behind or below what's correct. (Behind on what God is currently doing) If you read the twenty fourth chapter of St. Luke you'll find that Jesus was walking with them and he asked them what was everybody talking about. Cleopas said in so many words, man where've you been? Are you from another town? They killed Jesus, some say they saw angels and his body is gone. He said something about getting up in three days. (This is amazing because it shows you human nature) We're good at what we know but God is always doing something new because there's no limit on God. Some of us are just slow and need to catch up. (Say to yourself catch up) Jesus began to say didn't Moses and all the prophets expound on this in the scriptures. This is the same as when a prophet prophesies to you and you're slow to believe. 2 Chronicles 20:20 says, "Believe his prophets, so shall ye prosper." Jesus continued to walk with them reminding them of the prophetic word. St. Luke 24:31 says, "Their eyes were opened, and they knew him; and he vanished out of their sight." The bible says they rose, went to Jerusalem, found the eleven and testified of their experience and as they were speaking, Jesus himself stood in front of them and the bible says they were terrified and frightened. Jesus asked. Why are you frightened in your heart? Didn't they just testify about the experience they just had with Jesus? (I see why Jesus said slow of heart to believe) Some of you don't believe your own testimonies. (If Jesus did it once he'll do it again) Jesus went through the whole process of dealing with someone slow. Look at my feet, a spirit doesn't have flesh and bone. Look at my hands, give me something to eat, he even took them over the prophesies of Moses and what was written in the Psalms about him. Sometimes we're all a little slow but God is awesome and looks beyond our understanding and works with us until we catch up.

KEEP THE CONFIDENCE IN THE GOD IN YOUR LIFE

Job 32:1-3, "So these three men ceased to answer Job, because he was righteous in his own eyes. Then was kindled the wrath of Elihu the son of Barachel the Buzite, of the kindred of Ram: against Job was his wrath kindled, because he justified himself rather than God. Also against his three friends was his wrath kindled, because they had found no answer, and yet had condemned Job." Jobs family and friends judged him based on the trials he was going through but Job stood his ground in the mist of strong opposition because he had peace in the life he put before God. Elihu Felt he was the righteous among them so he spoke bold against Job and because he was the new young hot shot in God he felt as though he had the monopoly as he felt the God in his life was superior to Jobs. Elihu spoke bold against Job thinking he had such great insight concerning Jobs life but no one has greater insight in your life then you yourself. People will pass judgment on you quick because of their own self-righteous ways but you should not allow people to destroy your relationship with God because God measures the heart and God see's your true inner man. Elihu told Job he was old and that he himself was young and well-studied. Look at what the bible says in Job 31:8, 9 "But there is a spirit in man: and the inspiration of the Almighty giveth them understanding. Great men are not always wise: neither do the aged understand judgment." Listening to someone who can quote the word like that is enough to break down anybody's confidence but not Jobs. Anyone can be a tool used by Satan even a preacher if they aren't prayed up and balanced in God because the Satan will use the word and twist it to accomplish his goal but you must remember God wants to build you up and make you strong in the mist of your trial not condemn you. You know within yourself if you have done something wrong, if so repent. If you haven't done anything wrong stand like Job and wait till your change comes.

THE MENTORING TRAP

A mentor is an experienced, trusted adviser or trainer. Having a mentor to instruct you in the proper way whether it's through demonstration or coaching I believe is part of the cycle of life. Mentors pass on their secrets and experiences that may have taken a lifetime to achieve. Let's use a family recipe for example. The recipe can't be given or taught to just anyone it's usually a son or a daughter who is entrusted with the recipe and in most cases the ingredients aren't written down. The mentor teaches them the proper measurements of the ingredients, how to mix the ingredients, the art of hitting and molding the bread with their hands the same as great grandpa or great grandma did and how long to cook the dish. (This is how the taste stays the same down through the years) When the recipe is handed down to someone that's not a family member and cooking isn't in their genes, that's when you run into a problem. You see you been eating those cookies all your life but all of a sudden you eat one and say something is missing. (I'm just using this as an example) Let's talk about ministry. A son grows up watching his father's mannerisms, as well as listening to his father preach, how his father elevates his voice, his father's work ethic and style of dressing. The son is mentored to replace the father, so it's natural for the son because it's in his genes, plus he comes from a long line of ministers. Now there are other ministers in the same church that have been more faithful then the son to his father and more faithful to the church. They can mimic the father, dress like him, preach like him, and think like him but it didn't come natural. Their genes are from another man who is totally different from the man that they mimic and here is where you fall into the mentoring trap. Instead of eating the meat and spitting out the bones you swallow the whole thing and choke. Now you're disappointed in yourself but it's not in your genes to sing, preach and elevate your voice that way. Every time you try to sing you get hoarse and your throat becomes sore. Thank God that he saved you but don't lose your man trying to be someone that you're not. You diminish yourself when you're not true to yourself, so if you're a teacher teach because some men will take advantage of you and lock you in this trap. You must know that life changes from generation to generation and some men will steal your man right out of you by telling you you're not humble. I heard an overseer tell his ministers "They should think like their leader" My thoughts were they should think with the wisdom of God because the biblical guidelines should all have the same spirit. Yes a leader wants things a certain way and you should work with that parameter of understanding but circumstances sometimes arise and you can't ask yourself what your pastor would do because your pastor may have never faced that circumstance or particular situation. You need to depend on the wisdom of God and the training God has invested in you. God can't use you if you're thoughts are of another man. Remember any good leader wants someone who can think fast on their feet otherwise how can he expand his ministry. Just think about that for a moment. Why would your leader need someone that has to ask him everything? Understanding how your leader likes things done is one thing but not having your own freedom to make the best decision becomes a trap. Some leaders fill threatened by a person all because the person has master degrees in business and understands a different side of ministry, even though the person is working alongside them in the ministry on their behalf. I have found in my travels that some leaders are insecure, jealous and controlling. This is the reason why some ministries don't grow because they hinder each other through mimicking, confinement and control. When an animal is caught in a trap they will die if they can't get out. (If you are caught in the mentoring trap of ministry you will die out along with that ministry) Even if the animal does get out it will be scared and this is the same in ministry. So if you get caught in the mentoring trap find a way to escape. You will have a spiritual scare but you will live and the experience will work to your benefit as you will be able to help someone else.

ONLY THE ANOINTING

Isaiah 10:27, "And it shall come to pass in that day, that his burden shall be taken away from off thy shoulder, and his yoke from off the neck, and the yoke shall be destroyed because of the anointing." God has chosen people to do things other than preach. When you're ordained to do a job, you're already blessed because you're chosen or anointed for a certain purpose. There're certain people God have ordained to do certain things, and there's no compromise. You simply yield and obey or you don't: no matter what your intentions are. Have you ever wondered when you support a certain Man or Woman of God and they pray for you in your time of need, you get results? But when you turn or stop that support, things start to go the other way. If something is working why change it? The anointed is simply someone nominated or chosen for a position, a divine holy office; like a Priest, King or any other leader. In most cases there's usually a ceremony in which the chosen is anointed by the smearing or rubbing of oil. This seals that they've received the office, the calling and the responsibility that comes with that office. When God has preordained your life your path is sealed. The problem is most of you like the things of Satan. Whenever you allow anything that Satan controls to come in your presence, there's corruption and all corruption has to cleansed, removed or destroyed. You must understand that if you yield to what you know is right, you will be blessed. To many of you are fighting spirit with flesh but you can't fight spirit with flesh because spirit must be fought with spirit. This is why you must know something about being in the spirit. The more experience you have (meaning spending time in the spirit) under the anointing, the stronger you are in fighting in the spirit. The problem is most of you don't understand what the anointing means; let alone how to function under it. The anointing is a divine influence. It's a presence that comes on or over you. A lot of times when you hear the Man of God say, "I feel my help", he's talking about the anointing. When the anointing comes upon the anointed and the power of God is using them, miracles begin to happen. Blinded eyes open, people get out of wheelchairs and diseases are healed because the anointing rides on the spirit of God. It is the residue of his power in which no human can take the full strength of this power. The anointing is so strong and powerful in the supernatural that the human body can only take so much. The anointing is alive and it rest upon you like a coat or cloak. It chooses the chosen and it's all ordained by God himself. This is why when you see the anointing fall on Gods anointed, you should not sit in your seat but you should rush to the altar, so hands may be laid on you while the Man or Woman of God is under the anointing. Now this is not like a gift, because the Bible tells us in Romans 11:29, "For the gifts and calling of God are without repentance." God is not a reneging God. The gift that God placed in you stays with you, good or bad. But by the anointing being alive, it comes and goes as it pleases. You must work with the anointing and not against it. It never ceases to amaze me how people are trying to work in something they aren't anointed for. What you're anointed to do may not be as glorious as the next person, but it's just as important. When God chooses you, he will lead, guide and give you instructions. The problem is you tend to take charge yourself because you think God is too slow or that you know a better way. All because you want the limelight and the glitter, but if you're not anointed for something that leads you out front, people can tell and you embarrass yourself. So if God tells you something it's for a reason because God can see far into the future of your life. There was a man in the Bible named Manoah whose wife was barren. An angel of the Lord appeared unto her. Judges 13:5 says, "For, lo, thou shalt conceive, and bear a son; and no razor shall come on his head: for the child shall be a Nazarite unto God from the womb; and he shall begin to deliver Israel out of the hand of the Philistine." This child's name was Samson and as Samson grew up, the Bible says in the 25th verse, "And the spirit of the Lord began to move him at times in the camp." Meaning the anointing came upon Samson and he got use to it coming upon him. Judges 16:20 says, "And he awoke out of his sleep, and said, I will go out as at other times before and shake myself. And he wist not that the Lord was departed from him." Samson knew the secret to his strength and as long as he kept the secret, he was safe. But when Samson told his secret, the anointed spirit of God left. Yes the presence of God along with the anointing will leave you. You can try to function without it but you and everyone else will know that something is wrong, off and missing. Because you can't fake the presence of the anointing, it's either there or it isn't. You can hear a gifted singer sing and its good but when you hear a gifted singer singing under the anointing it will break and penetrate your spirit because it moves you emotionally. If you lose the presence of the anointing you can get it back, just repent and stop doing whatever made it depart from you. Samson did and when he was restored he took three thousand with him in his death. This is real and God is not playing.

HAPPY HOLIDAYS

As the holidays approach there're many different beliefs and opinions. But there's one thing for sure, you can feel good will and that, we will take at any time. The Bible says in Romans 14:5-8, "One man esteemeth one day above another: another esteemeth every day alike. Let every man be fully persuaded in his own mind. He that regardeth the day regardeth it unto the Lord; and he that regardeth not the day, to the Lord he doeth not regard it. He that eateth, eateth to the Lord, for he giveth God thanks; and he that eateth not, to the Lord he eateth not, and giveth God thanks. For none of us liveth to himself, and no man dieth to himself. For whether we live, we live unto the Lord; whether we die, we die unto the Lord: whether we live therefore, or die, we are the Lords." So enjoy these festive days giving God the glory in all that you do. Give God thanks that things are as well as they are in his grace and mercy. You must appreciate Gods presence with respect and monitor what you allow in your presence because as a child of light your space should carry the presence of God.

Whenever you enter a place people will feel the peace and the presence of God when you walk in and the children of darkness will become uncomfortable in the mist of your space. I understand the holiday season is not a happy season for everyone. In some cases the holiday season can be a sad time for those who've had bad experiences or the loss of a love one. No one can truly say they know how you feel because some have experienced more than others. But you must live on and find your way back to good will. Because evil will try to feed on those negative emotions and lure you into a deep depression, where demons are waiting to destroy you. So don't treat the presence of God like it's cheap or unimportant. Because the presence of God is nothing to play with! 1st Chronicles 13:14 says, "And the ark of God remained with the family of Obed-edom in his house three months. And the Lord blessed the house Obed-edom, and all that he had." Let's look at what happened to Uzza in the same chapter verses 7-10, "And they carried the ark of God in a new cart out of the house of Abinadab: and Uzza and Ahio drove the cart. And David and all Israel played before God with all their might, and with singing, and with harps, and with psalteries, and with timbrels, and with cymbals, and with trumpets. And when they came unto the threshing floor of Chidon, Uzza put forth his hand to hold the ark; for the oxen stumbled. And the anger of the Lord was kindled against Uzza, and he smote him, because he put his hand to the ark: and there he died before God." The presence of God was with the ark. When the presence of God is in any place blessings come with it, as long as you obey the will of God and his instructions. Uzza was ordained and chosen to drive the cart. But he was not to touch the ark because

Levites were forbidden to touch the ark on threat of death. God has certain people he's ordained to do certain things and there's no compromising. Though Uzza intentions were honorable, they were against the rules of God. God has rules no matter what your intentions are; he is bound by his word. This is a great example of how you can lose focus during the holiday festivities and become disobedient to what God has told you. So stay with the flow and allow the fullness of the presence of God to work through your life and allow your life to be blessed.

Printed in the United States
By Bookmasters